BELIEF REPORTS AND THE STRUCTURE OF BELIEVING

IN MEMORIAM · PHILIP K. HENRY · AMAVIT · SOPHIAM ET CATOS

1952   1987

Belief Reports

and the
Structure of Believing

Philip R. Henry

Foreword by
Julius Moravcsik and John Perry

CSLI Publications
Center for the Study of Language
and Information
Stanford, California

Copyright © 1998
CSLI Publications
Center for the Study of Language and Information
Leland Stanford Junior University
Printed in the United States
02 01 00 99 98   5 4 3 2 1

Library of Congress Cataloging-in-Publication Data
Henry, Philip R. 1952–
Belief reports and the structure of believing / Philip Henry.
p. cm.
Includes bibliographical references and index.
ISBN 1–57586–141–0 (hardcover : alk. paper).
ISBN 1–57586–140–2 (pbk. : alk. paper)
1. Belief and doubt. I. Title.
BD215.H457 1997
121'.6—dc21
97–40512
CIP

The frontispiece, from which the detail on the front cover of the paperback edition of this book was derived, was designed by the Turtle's Quill Scriptorium of Medocino, California.

FOREWORD

The present essay constitutes the core of the philosophical work of Phillip R. Henry. It was left unfinished because of his untimely death in 1987. Henry's essay weaves together concerns from three different literatures in philosophy: the logical analysis of propositional attitude reports (Quine), the semantics and metaphysics of cognition (Fodor, Putnam, Burge), and issues of causation and externalism in epistemology (Gettier, Goldman, Lehrer). The topics these literatures deal with fit naturally together, but the literatures do not. Often ideas are developed in one in isolation form the others; sometimes authors in one area see the relevance of the others, but do not have the patience to get things straight.

Henry proceeds logically and carefully from a penetrating study of Quine's seminal distinction between notional and relational attitude reports, to a careful study of methodological solipsism, to an analysis of the place of a theory of cognitive content within epistemology. Henry sees important distinctions, and illustrates them with apt examples. If his final position, Weak Cognitive Individualism, is somewhat complex, the complexity is well grounded in solid, well-argued distinctions.

Ten years after Henry's death, it seems to us that the confusions that Henry argued against are still common, the distinctions he drew still valuable, and his overall vision of how current work in cognition and semantics and traditional concerns of epistemology might fit together still extremely helpful to those wishing to understand the interplay among these three literatures. It has seemed worthwhile then to make his ideas available to a wider audience.

The present essay is based on the version of the dissertation he left. We have omitted some unfinished sections, and eliminated some references to them in other parts. The citations were unfinished; we have listed at the end the works of the authors Henry mentions that he most likely had in mind. We are grateful to CSLI Publications for helping us in making Henry's ideas more widely available.

Henry entered the Stanford Philosophy Department Ph.D. program in September, 1977. He passed his orals in February, 1982. He died on December 2, 1987. The memorial service was held on December 16, 1987. Henry was a serious and talented philosopher, whose ideas influenced other members of the department, both students and faculty. He was hard at work on his dissertation at the time of his death. Moravcsik was his advisor, and Perry a member of his committee.

Julius Moravcsik
John Perry

CONTENTS

Foreword   v

Introduction   1

Part I   15

Psychology, Cognition, and the Individual   17

Part II   41

Epistemic Values and Epistemic Stratification   43

References   101

Name Index   103

INTRODUCTION

1.0

We may distinguish two major varieties of belief reports—the opaque and the transparent. We may also distinguish two principal types of beliefs which pertain to individuals or individual roles—the general and the particular. These distinctions must not be conflated. They may conceivably be regarded as parallel distinctions, as in a prescriptive code of belief attribution, but they need not. On the one hand we have a set of logical and linguistic questions, and on the other, a set of epistemological questions. In W.V. Quine's seminal article (Quine 1956) he fails to discuss adequately any connection between the two sets of questions, and concentrates upon the logical questions. I intend to deal primarily with the epistemological questions, arguing that there are indeed two important varieties of believing regarding individual objects—not merely two varieties of belief reports differing in their logical properties.

1.1

Traditionally, the complement sentences occurring in ascriptions of propositional attitudes have been treated as referentially opaque; i.e., singular denoting expressions in such sentences have been thought not in general to be subject to the logical operations of coextensional substitution and existential generalization. These are operations which are recognized to be valid except within these and other special contexts (notably contexts governed by alethic modal operators). Thus from most statements of the form '$F(a)$' where 'F' is any predicate and 'a' any singular term, the inference to '$(E\ x)(F(x))$' is a valid one; and so, together with the premise '$a=b$,' is the inference to '$F(b)$.' However from a statement of the form

1

(1)   *S* believes that *G(a)*

and the additional premise '*a=b*', it is, in general, invalid to infer

(2)   *S* believes that *G(b)*;

and, as the laws of substitutivity of identicals (SI) and existential generalization (EG) presumably stand or fall together, the inference from (1) to

(3)   (E *x*)(*S* believes that *G(x)*)

is likewise invalid.

The traditional reluctance to allow unrestricted substitution of codesignative singular terms within belief contexts, and unrestricted existential quantification into such contexts, may probably be seen to rest upon the traditional albeit often tacit acceptance of some such principle as

(A)   A believing subject has cognitive access to what he believes; i.e., knows what it is that he believes, so that if a subject in fact holds a belief that *P*, any reflective denial on his part that *P* is the case, or profession of suspension of belief regarding whether or not *P* is the case, must be insincere.

To accept (A) is to be committed to the view that a subject is invariably an infallible (or very nearly infallible) authority on what it is that he himself believes. Now every subject is inevitably ignorant, with respect to any individual object, of many of the names and singular descriptions of that object. Therefore there must be many belief reports, for any believing subject and individual object, obtained by substitution, in virtue of an identity statement of which the subject is ignorant, from a belief report to which the subject would assent. Such belief reports will be sincerely and reflectively denied by the subject, and so, on principle (A), are false; but if substitution of coextensional terms, and existential generalization, are valid for belief contexts, then such reports are all true.

By way of example, if (1) is true and *S* assents to it, but *S* is ignorant of the identity statement '*a=b*,' then *S* will sincerely and reflectively deny (2). Thus by (A), (2) is false; but if belief contexts are referentially transparent, then by (1) together with the identity statement, (2) is true. Hence if (A) is true, belief contexts are referentially opaque.

We do indisputably employ sentences ascribing propositional attitudes, in which an existential quantifier outside the context of the propositional attitude verb binds variables occurring within that context. Thus we may say, e.g.,

(4)   There is someone whom my sister believes to be a fascist.

This ascription is undeniably of that form, yet locutions are to be found in ordinary language which may be ambiguous as between the quantified-into ascription and the unquantified-into ascription. Consider, for example,

(5)   My sister believes that someone is a fascist.

Its ambiguity as between (4) and

(6)   My sister believes there to be fascists

is not difficult to feel, especially if we append 'here' or another appropriate modifier to 'someone'.

Given the normal propensity to treat doxastic (and other propositional attitude) contexts as referentially opaque, the use of ascription sentences into which we quantify existentially from without presents a substantive problem. Clearly, (3) is not derived straightforwardly from (1) if belief contexts are indeed opaque. The first important attempt to deal with this problem is by W.V. Quine (1956). He wishes "to provide for those indispensable relational statements of belief, like 'There is someone whom Ralph believes to be a spy'." (To "relational" statements he contrasts notional statements of belief.) That such quantification-in "is a dubious business" he illustrates by means of the familiar anecdote wherein Ralph, the believing subject, suspects a certain man, whom Ralph has seen on several occasions wearing a brown hat, of being a spy; yet there is also a gray-haired man, whom Ralph knows to be named Ortcutt and has seen once at the beach, whom Ralph believes to be anything but a spy. Unbeknownst to Ralph, these are the same man; the man in the brown hat is Ortcutt. Now if we can correctly regard Ralph's believing him to be a spy as a property of the man Ortcutt, i.e., if Ralph stands in the relation to Ortcutt himself of believing him to be a spy; then we seemingly must concede that Ralph believes that Ortcutt is a spy, even though Ralph sincerely denies 'Ortcutt is a spy'. However if principle (A) or an equivalent principle of access is maintained then we must reject the statement that Ralph believes that Ortcutt is a spy, and must affirm both

(7)   Ralph believes that the man in the brown hat is a spy

and

(8)   Ralph does not believe that the man at the beach (Ortcutt) is a spy.

Thus there appears to be a dilemma to be resolved. The first resolution Quine suggests is the distinguishing of two different senses of the verb 'believe', $belief_1$, which is the opaque sense, and $belief_2$, the transparent sense. Belief reports in which the verb is used in the second sense are reports for which all coextensional substitution and, existential quantification is permissible. It is true, then, that Ralph believes$_2$ that Ortcutt is a spy, in virtue of the truth of (7); and supposing that Ralph not only fails to believe that the man at the beach is a spy (which could be merely a case of suspended belief) but firmly believes that the man seen at the beach is *not* a spy, it is also true that Ralph believes$_2$ that Ortcutt is not a spy! The conjunction of these two $belief_2$ reports, however, does not in itself impute irrationality to Ralph: he is not guilty of believing a contradiction; he is merely ignorant of the relevant identity statement, although the $belief_2$ reports conceal the exact nature of his ignorance nonetheless. $Belief_1$ reports are such that the subject's sincere (and reflective) denial of a report suffices to falsify it. Quine stipulates, furthermore, that $belief_1$ reports quantified from without are nonsense.

Quine goes on to advance a more sophisticated proposal, that of adopting, for the purposes of technical discussion, a single belief-predicate with a variable number of argument places (with two as the lower limit). The first argument place is occupied by a name (or description) of the believing subject; the second is occupied by the name of an intension of degree n, and the remaining n places (if any) are occupied by singular denoting expressions, all of which occur in purely referential position. Intensions of degree 0 are propositions, those of degree 1 are attributes, and so forth. Tokens of the belief predicate which have only two argument places relate the subject to a proposition; those with three relate the subject to an attribute and an individual object; those with more than three relate the subject to an intension of degree n and n individuals. As an example of a report in which the predicate has two argument places, Quine offers

(9)   Ralph believes that Ortcutt is a spy,

and as an example of a report in which it has three,

(10)   Ralph believes z (z is a spy) of Ortcutt.

It is illegitimate to perform extensional transformations on names of intensions. They constitute the only *parts* of belief contexts (subcontexts, if you will) which are, on this treatment, referentially opaque. Singular terms occurring outside of names of intensions may be validly existentially generalized, and coextensional terms may be validly substituted for them.

The advantage of this treatment over the *belief₁/belief₂* approach becomes apparent for those cases in which the name of the intension contains a singular term:

(11)   Tom believes y (y was denounced by Tully) of Catiline.

From (11) it cannot be validly inferred that

(12)   Tom believes y (y was denounced by Cicero) of Catiline.

(11) affirms a relationship between Tom and Catiline and an attribute—and not between Tom and the individual Tully (Cicero) at all. Neither a *belief₁* report relating Tom to a complete proposition, nor a *belief₂* report in which the name 'Cicero' occurs in purely referential position, enjoys the precision of (9), which relates Tom to (an intension and) one and only one individual.

Somewhere beneath the surface of Quine's discussion runs a murky current of epistemological and general cognitive-scientific interest. One is led to wonder whether propositional attitudes themselves, and not only senses of propositional attitude attributions, may be classified as relational or notional. Are there indeed certain types of relationships in which a subject may stand to an individual, which constitute his beliefs about that individual as of a special, "relational" kind? Quine at one point writes of "dyadic belief" and "triadic belief" as though these were two separate epistemological phenomena. It is mildly surprising that he does not discuss any such special relations as needing to obtain in each case in which a relational belief report is, strictly speaking, true. There is even reason to doubt whether he feels that any investigation would be philosophically profitable in which such a relation were sought.

The logical operation in which a singular term is moved out of the name of an intension in a belief report and into purely referential position to form a now report, Quine calls "exportation." Any such new report has an additional argument place in the belief predicate. He claims that "the kind of exportation which leads from (9) to (10) should doubtless be viewed in general as implicative." By 'the kind of exportation....' he presumably means exportation in general, but what is meant by 'implicative' here is problematic. It is certainly reasonable to suppose that he means that every correct instance of the transformation carries with it the implication of some further condition (such as a special epistemic relationship between the subject and the denotatum of the term) being fulfilled. David Kaplan and Tyler Burge construe Quine's statement as a pronouncement that exportation is a logically valid operation. This would be a puzzling claim for him to makes inasmuch as the referential opacity of names of intensions would by its truth be rendered trivial: the prohibition against quantifying or substituting into a sentence like (9) would seem to amount to nothing, since it would be feasible to infer (10) directly from (9) and then to quantify or substitute into (10).

1.2

Any study of this kind must take care to distinguish two issues, one primarily logical and linguistic, the other primarily epistemological. Quine has addressed himself to the logical question, namely

I.   Whether and under what conditions it is acceptable and intelligible to treat singular terms occurring in belief attributions as terms in referential positions.

This involves inquiring what sense is to be made of belief reports in which substitution, or existential quantification from outside the belief context, has been performed on one or more terms inside that context. He has left open the epistemological questions viz.,

II.   Whether there are actually two kinds of believing about particular concrete objects—one wherein the subject stands in a special cognitive relationship to the object, another in which no such relationship obtains and the belief is about the object only in virtue of the subject's use of certain concepts.

Quine has not addressed this questions probably because he despairs of finding any difference in behavioral conditions distinguishing two such types of believing. He denies that the theory of propositional attitude attribution that is developed in the course of his discussion "is just a matter of allowing unbridled quantification into belief contexts after all, with a legalistic change of notation." It is left to the reader to decide just when and where terms in belief contexts are to be treated as purely referential: "Quantify if you will, but pay the price of accepting near-contraries like (10) and (13) [Ralph believes z (z is not a spy) of Ortcutt] at each point at which you choose to quantify." It might seem most natural to choose to treat terms in belief contexts as purely referential when and only when they designate individuals to which the subject stands in a special relationship (e.g., of acquaintance) which distinguishes *relational* belief (whatever exactly that may be); hence that each reader wishing to affirm a distinction between two fundamentally different varieties of believing should antecedently settle upon the nature of the special relation, then quantify (or not) accordingly. But we shall see that it is wrong to assume without argument the connection between these two issues to be such that referential occurrence of terms in belief contexts must reflect relationality of beliefs, and thus such that if the notion of relational belief is an empty or incoherent one the referential occurrence of such terms is not allowable. In fact, *no* logical connection between I and II should be assumed from the start.

It has been assumed throughout the foregoing discussion that the extensional inferences are, where valid, valid together, and where invalid, invalid together; that in general, existential generalization is not allowed where coextensional substitution is banned— nor is substitution permissible anywhere existential generalization is forbidden. To treat these two kinds of transformations differently may well be unusual and ill-advised, but it is not altogether incoherent. Recall that Quine's primary goal in (1956) was to make sense of propositional attitude reports existentially quantified from without. Yet the difficulties arose as a consequence of permitting unlimited coextensional substitution rather than solely in connection with quantifying-in itself. Why not seek to avoid the embarrassment of accepting "near-contraries" like (10) and (13) by allowing quantifying-in while retaining a prohibition against substitution? Perhaps a more natural setting for the segregating of these two extensional inference patterns would employ a *substitutional* interpretation of externally bound variables within intensional contexts in contradistinction to the ordinary objectual interpretation. In this way opacity may be strictly observed while definite sense is accorded to the quantified-into reports. A sentence of the form of (3) would be true on this construal just in case some sentence of the form of (1) were true.

1.3

To answer question II affirmatively does not require that one share many doctrines, or share much of a broad philosophical point of view, with any others who answer it affirmatively. The development of an affirmative answer typically consists of two main strands.

One is a characterization (ideally both clear and exact) of each of the two genera of belief being postulated, with emphasis upon the contrast between them. The other is the argumentation presented in favor of the correctness of the picture being presented—why the principles according to which the distinction is drawn are the appropriate ones, and why the line of demarcation between the two genera should be a prominent feature in the anatomy of belief. The two strands are, as may be expected, virtually inseparable.

The terms 'relational' and 'notional', as used above to designate varieties of belief, will now be abandoned in favor of 'particular' and 'general', respectively; for, as will gradually become manifest, the latter pair better captures the major structural asymmetry in cognition with respect to individual objects. Probably the pair of labels most widely used for the purpose are *'de re'* and *'de dicto'*—which are also applied to modal statements about individuals. I decline to use them, for two reasons. In the first place *'de dicto'* means literally 'of or about what is said'; more to the point is 'about the concept', an alternative sense in which *'de dicto'* is frequently taken. The truly serious inadequacy of the term *'de dicto'* lies in the fact that not all general beliefs are framed entirely in words or concepts: there are those, I argue later, which are in part composed of unarticulated sensory information. Now *'de re'* I take as an acceptable synonym of 'particular' in the current context, and I will sometimes use it as such. However—and this is my second reason—the pair *'de re/de dicto'* has been used very widely, and has been forced to bear the weight of a great many different technical senses. It may therefore be suspected of insidiously bringing in undesirable connotations.

Some methodological remarks are in order. First, the two genera of believing are distinguished by the two types of belief contents we will call "general" and "particular." It is held that the difference in structures of contents underlies a difference in the structure of the phenomenon of believing. This is established by evoking a contrast between the conditions of believing a general content and those of believing a particular content. Our picture of the two genera of belief will represent them as being mutually exclusive, and hence neither will be reducible to the other. Intuitions regarding distinctness of kinds of believing will be appealed to, but only to demonstrate that, pretheoretically, we recognize certain instances of believing to be clearly general and not about the (denoted) object in any interesting sense, and other instances to be directly about the relevant individual. A felt contrast in aboutness of beliefs is one of the more or less intuitive contrasts that will be rather useful. Russell's distinction between knowledge (of objects) by acquaintance and by description is another; and yet a third pertains to the question whether the identity of the given object is essential or accidental to the identity of the believed content.

The question whether a belief or other attitude is about an individual is of course extremely vague. There are certainly many ways in which, and many degrees to which, a belief may be about an object. However a strict and narrow sense of 'about' may be distinguished which does not admit of degrees. Let us say a belief is *n-about* an object *x* just in case the identity of *x* is an essential part of the content believed. It is also worthwhile to recognize a very wide sense of 'about': we may say that a belief is *w-about x* if and only if a correct articulation of the content incorporates an expression that only contingently denotes *x*.

Calling what is believed the content of belief has its advantages and disadvantages. Among the former are the general acceptance of this usage and the avoidance of the unwanted associations that may attach to the alternatives. Colloquially, what one believes is ordinarily called simply one's "belief," but the abstract substantive term 'belief' is ambiguous as between that which is believed and the act of believing it. Some philosophers, notably John Perry, prefer to refer to what is believed as the "object of belief." In the context of a discussion of beliefs pertaining to individual objects, that usage is not entirely apposite, for, in the first places whatever is believed is of the category of entities which, if true, may be known; and 'object of one's knowledge' is most readily construed as 'individual with which one is acquainted'. Thus, since it is more common to use 'object' to mean 'entity' or 'substance' than to mean 'denotatum of a grammatical object', it is much too easy to interpret 'object of a belief' as 'individual about which a belief is held' in one or another sense of 'about'.

The chief disadvantage in our use of 'content' lies in its heredity. Russell used the terms 'what is believed' and 'content of belief' interchangeably. However his conception of content was, following Meinong, that of psychological content—content of consciousness—rather than that of semantic content. Semantic content is, as we shall see, the notion that is appropriate here. For Russell, belief was very much a mental or psychological phenomenon: of the three elements in his analysis of belief—the act of believing, what is believed (content), and the objective—the first two were thoroughly psychological in nature. The remaining element, the objective, was for Russell the fact that makes the belief true or false. We shall see, perhaps most clearly by examining relational (i.e., *particular*) beliefs and the conditions of holding them, that no purely psychological account of the holding of beliefs can be adequate. Specifically, what is believed cannot be constituted solely of contents of consciousness, for then belief could be analyzed as a relation between the subject and purely mental entities.

Why should what is believed be assimilated to semantic content? Primarily because belief contents are either true or false, i.e., are assessable for truth value. Truth and falsity are semantical notions whether or not one's theory of semantics posits as references of statements the "objects" The True and The False. The paradigm case of bearers of truth values should be complete statements rather than sentences, since not all sentences have truth values outside of contexts of utterance or inscription. What statements *express* we may, call semantic contents, and these as well as the statements themselves may be viewed as being true or false. Semantic contents of this specific type are frequently called *propositions*, both in Fregean semantic theories and in such non-Fregean semantic theories as that of Jon Barwise and John Perry. (Barwise and Perry, 1983). Propositions are not restricted, I shall argue, to those entities which linguistic statements can be formulated to express in an exact fashion. Whatever propositions—i.e., those items that are either true or false and that may be believed—turn out to be, we should recognize a relatively uncontroversial theoretical constraint on their nature: viz., intersubjective accessibility. No proposition may be such that it cannot in principle be believed or entertained by any subject possessing sufficiently acute cognitive powers. This amounts mainly to the repudiation of the notion that propositions may be essentially private.

Propositions which exhibit n-aboutness to an individual x we will call *particular with respect to x*, and those only. All others that are about x at all (i.e., at least w-about x) we will call *general with respect to x*. The two classes, of propositions that are particular with respect to some object, and those that are general with respect to some object, are not disjoint: if indeed there are actual beliefs and other propositional attitudes whose contents fall into each category, we should expect to find contents to be believed which, for some distinct individuals x and y, are particular with respect to x and general with respect to y. The concept of a multiplicity of possible worlds is helpful in formulating explicitly and clearly the particular/general distinction for propositions. The truth, at any possible world W, of the particular proposition that b is F, depends only upon b's being F in W. A general proposition that the D is F, on the other hand, is true in those and only those worlds in which exactly one D exists, and that individual is F. It is irrelevant to the truth condition of a general proposition which individual the proposition happens to be about in a given world—i.e., *which* individual would be inspected with the purpose of verifying or falsifying the proposition in that world—but it alone must possess the attribute D in that world. No commitment to a semantics of possible worlds is needed in understanding the distinction in this way; nevertheless it is assumed that it is coherent to speak of an actual individual's existing in a counterfactual situation.

If b is the D in actuality, and if b is F, then both the particular proposition that b is F and the general proposition that the D is F are true. The latter is true not in virtue of the F-ness of b as the former is, but in virtue of the fact that something is both F and uniquely D. It will be false (assuming that its truth is contingent) in some worlds in which b is F—i.e., in which the particular proposition is true. Similarly, the particular proposition will be false in certain worlds in which the general proposition is true—viz., wherever b fails to be either F or D, and some other entity is uniquely D and is F. Note that the two propositions are materially equivalent, however: their truth values coincide at the actual world.

Sentences containing definite descriptions are notably ambiguous as between expressing general and singular propositions, although the ambiguity is most apparent in descriptions within nonextensional contexts. The first important analysis of definite descriptions was provided by Russell, and his distinction between their primary and secondary occurrences serves to explain the ambiguity. The definite description, being ambiguous, suggests a relation of correspondence between the two alternative propositions it may express. We shall say that the particular proposition which may be expressed, in any specified world, by a sentence containing a definite description, *corresponds* in that world to the general proposition expressed by that sentence (which is w-about only one individual). To any general proposition there corresponds at any world at most one particular proposition. Yet every particular proposition has a great variety of general propositions to which it corresponds. To accommodate the possibility that there are general propositions—and particular propositions as well—that are not linguistically expressible, this correspondence relation should be defined without reference to linguistic articulations of the relata. The definition must focus, in other words, upon the objects that general propositions are w-about and that particular propositions are n-about. General propositions of the (unarticulated) sort at issue must consist of one or more parcels of general content which uniquely pick out individuals—e.g., individuating images—as well as some general content(s) predicated of the individuals. Particular propositions may be understood either to contain individuals themselves as components, or else to contain non-descriptive concepts of some kind which uniquely pick out individuals. At any rate, the correspondence relation holds at a world W between a general proposition P and a particular proposition P whenever i) the objects picked out in P at W are the same, and occurring in the same order, as those occurring in, or picked out by, P' at W; and ii) the attributes predicated of the respective objects, and the relations in which they are asserted to stands are the same in P' as in P.

PART I

Psychology, Cognition, and the Individual

Traditionally, propositional attitudes, including, most of those attitudes that are, properly speaking, cognitive (i.e., belief, doubt, wonder—everything but knowledge) have been viewed as though they were purely psychological in character. On this view, pervasive in modern and contemporary philosophy, and in psychology, to believe (doubt, wonder, etc.) that P, is simply to be in a certain psychological state type—a state type that is instantiated by all and only those subjects who believe (doubt, etc.) that P. The most interesting version of this view is slightly weaker, and will become in this section the official reference of 'psychologism'. Another thesis, also widely held at least since Descartes—viz. that psychological states are entirely internal to the subject—finds more or less definitive expression in a formulation of Methodological Solipsism (henceforth "MS"). These theses, MS and psychologism, conjoined, constitute the position I shall call "Narrow Psychologism in Cognitive Theory" (henceforth "NPC"). It will be demonstrated that NPC is untenable, and I will maintain that psychologism, rather than MS, is the culprit.

In practicing "folk psychology," as we all do, we explain and predict behavior of ourselves and others—usually with an appreciable measure of success. We attribute motivational and cognitional states to individual agents and depict various bits or patterns of behavior each as the resultant of some constellation of such states. It is perfectly unsurprising that most of the states so attributed are just propositional attitudes. Given an adequate list of an agent's beliefs, desires, intentions, doubts, aversions, etc., a great deal of his past behavior becomes intelligible, and much of his future behavior becomes foreseeable, at least conditionally so. At a common-sense level of psychological explanation, then, propositional attitudes are, paradigmatically, psychological states. At this level, to believe that *P* is to be in a psychological state type shared by all and only those who believe that *P*; and similarly for all other kinds of propositional attitudes.

There is thus undeniably a common conception of the psychological according to which propositional attitudes are straightforwardly psychological phenomena. This is a conception that we shall have reason to reject. It is not conducive to theoretical economy and will be superseded by a conception that is preferable for the purposes of empirical psychology and (phenomenology) alike. Now it is perhaps false that two subjects can hold *all* of their propositional attitudes in common and yet exhibit significantly different propensities to behave. But, we shall see, one difference in attitude contents between two subjects S_1 and S_2 (e.g., that they hold exactly the same total set of cognitive attitudes except that, whereas S_1 believes Ps_1, S_2 believes P_2, P_1 and P_2 being distinct propositions) may in principle clearly fail to effect any difference (possible or actual) in their entire behavioral histories. Serious doubt may thus be cast on the hypothesis that the content-discrepancy between them can amount to a genuine difference in (properly individuated) psychological state types.

The rest of the present section will be devoted to the refutation of NPC, and in the next, a defense of a form of MS (on grounds of theoretical economy) will be given, thus refuting psychologism simpliciter.

Jerry Fodor is the chief proponent of MS in cognitive psychology. The definitive statement of his views occurs in the paper "Methodological Solipsism Considered as a Research Strategy in Cognitive Psychology" (henceforth "MSCRS"). Credit for the current usage of the term 'methodological solipsism' belongs to Hilary Putnam, and Fodor follows Putnam's usage fairly closely. Putnam first introduced this term in his influential paper "The Meaning of 'Meaning,'" defining it as

> the assumption that no psychological state, properly so called, presupposes the existence of any individual other than the subject to whom the state is ascribed. [p.20]

He speaks correlatively of psychological states "in the narrow sense," "in the wide sense," distinguishing the latter as state types that would be disallowed by the assumption of MS, and the former as those that would be allowed. The latter are, from the point of view of MS, psychological states of an impure sort (such as "x's being jealous of y," which entails y's existence), combining genuine psychological states (in the narrow sense) with collateral, non-psychological details of the subject's situation.

Fodor develops MS as a conjunction of two doctrines—the representational theory of mind, and a "Formality Condition" on the theoretical postulation of cog-psychological state types. A picture of psychological states and processes as *computational* motivates this conjuction. The intuitive conviction underlying MS is that the psychological states of a subject, and the mental operations he undergoes, are constituted as they are independently of the disposition of his causal and social environment—that the states a subject is in, and the processes he undergoes, do not fully determine their "external" occasions. This view is eminently compatible with the denial of psychologism in cognitive attitude theory, although Fodor's discussion goes somewhat astray by failing to make this compatibility clear.

Fodor states the representational theory (which is actually more of a vague structural constraint on conceptions of the mental) as the constitution of mental, i.e., (cog-psychological) states by the instantiation of relations between individual *subjects* and *representations*. For a subject to be in a mental state of a specified type, on this theory, is for him to stand in a specific relation to a specific representation; neither more nor less. The type-identity of the state is a function of the relation and the representation type: subject S's standing in relation R to representation b would place S in a state of the same type as that in which any other subject S' would be in virtue of standing in R to b. It is taken by Fodor as quite natural that the "relations" in question be construed as varieties of propositional attitudes; he cites thinking, hoping, doubting, supposing, and pretending as examples. Such a construal strongly suggests the view that the representations in question would themselves typically be propositions. Psychologism would thus be all but inescapable, since each ordered pair consisting of a proposition and an attitude type would define a psychological state (type). For, a subject S's standing in the relation of *doubting* to the proposition *Some crows are white* would place S in a mental state of a definite type—call it T; similarly, any other subject S' who doubts that some crows are white will thereby be in a state of type T as well. Fortunately an alternative construal, one that does not entail psychologism is suggested by the Formality Condition and the psychological model that it serves: the representations should be taken to be syntactic (or other symbolic) entities which can *express* propositions, through semantic links which may vary according to context of use. The relations would then not be propositional attitude types, but sentential counterparts of those types, as accepting a sentence, in Perry's sense, is the counterpart of believing a proposition.

The Formality Condition (FC) is the stipulation that mental operations or processes are *formal* processes—i.e., that they are definable in strictly formal terms. More specifically, that they are definable as operations on certain items, each of which exhibits its own individual form, but which possess contents as well and that their definitions must contain no reference to particular contents. (We may best temporarily refrain from asking what these contents may be—phenomenological, semantic, etc.) As mental states and representations are the items upon which mental operations are performed, definitions of such operations, over the domain of mental states and representations must be formulable with reference only to the formal properties of these entities. To understand even vaguely what these formal properties might be, consider that, in line with the hypothesis that there is an inner code or language of thought (aka "Mentalese"), most of the representations at issue are to be regarded as syntactic entities. Their formal properties are exactly their syntactic properties. And, taking perceptual and memory images as another Fodorian example of representations, it is easily imaginable that some of their formal properties may be, e.g., shape and orientation.

An important consequence follows from the conjunction of FC with the representational theory, with respect to mental state—and representation-identity. Mental processes operate just on the formal properties of states and representations; these processes account for all efficient causation in the mental realm, being the vehicles of all generation and change of mental states and representations. Since these states and representations are theoretical entities—unobservable posits whose sole *raison d'être* is their role in a nomological model of behavior (at a non-physiological level)—their principle of individuation must be concerned exclusively with their regular roles in the causation of actual and possible behaviors. Distinct representations (or states) must have distinct causal roles. They enter these causal relations only as they are subjected to the mental operations, in virtue of having such formal properties as are specified in the definitions of the operations in question. Thus they are to be individuated strictly on the basis of their formal properties. To restate the foregoing, mental processes are blind, as it were, to any but the formal properties of representations, and since the principle of representation-individuation is nomological in nature representations are distinct if and only if they are distinct in the eyes of the processes. Similarly, two token mental *states* are of the same type just in case they place their subject(s) in the same kind of relation to formally identical representations.

In yoking FC to the representational theory, the notion of a representation employed becomes very clearly that of an uninterpreted symbol, or a symbol that fails to have its semantic interpretation, if any, essentially. This seems unusual. A representation is normally regarded as being essentially of that object (or property, etc.) which it represents. If *r* is any kind of representation of an item *x*—pictorial, iconic, linguistic, etc.—one tends to view *r* as having been produced or designated intentionally to represent *x*; and to be therefore, insofar as it *is* a representation, essentially a representation of *x*. A mental representation in Fodor's formal sense must be viewed otherwise—viz., as a symbol that is not intrinsically interpreted, but that is susceptible of various semantic interpretations. Thus there is a radical kind of bracketing of the semantic that is imposed by FC.

Underlying the commitment, on Fodor's part, to FC, is a computational approach to cognitive psychology. Mental processes are assimilated to computational processes carried out by means of manipulation of symbols. Fodor maintains that we may

> construe mental operations as pretty directly analogous to those of a Turing machine. [Mental functioning involves] a working memory (corresponding to a tape) and there are capacities for scanning and altering the contents of the memory (corresponding to the operations of reading and writing on the tape).

The senses can be thought of as transducers which enter information from the physical environment into the memory.

Computational processes, in general, are formal in character. This is easy to see in the case of artificial computing machines, i) because specific operations performed by such machines can be defined purely formally (i.e., mechanically); and ii) because the semantic interpretations assigned to symbols manipulated by computers are ultimately determined only by the intentional nature of the computational work a machine is being employed by a user to perform. If mental processes are indeed computational, then they must be formal. No real consideration of the adequacy of the computational model need be undertaken here, however. I will instead endeavor to frame MS in a more general form, one not vulnerable to the criticisms that may be directed against computational psychology per se. First I will show the incompatibility of Fodorian MS with psychologism; subsequently I will show the same incompatibility to hold between psychologism and generic MS.

Let us consider three pairs of possible belief scenarios—A, B_1, and B_2. In A a contrast ostensibly fatal for NPC will be drawn between beliefs of two subjects, and in B_1 and B_2 appropriately similar contrasts will be recognized where a single subject is involved and either 1) temporal or 2) possible world indices are varied. First, we have two normal subjects, call them Sandy and Chris (names chosen to leave gender indeterminate) who are cognitively very similar—i.e., have similar beliefs, memories, conceptual competencies, behavioral dispositions, etc. Since this is a thought experiment we are free to make them functionally exactly similar, if this be requisite to the persuasiveness of the example. We catch them at time t in separate, qualitatively indistinguishable rooms, each taking a long glance at a chair and declaring "That chair is an antique." Chair c_1, in Sandy's room, looks exactly like c_2, in Chris's room—but whereas c_1 is a genuine antique, c_2 is a recent, ingeniously constructed, facsimile. Neither Chris nor Sandy would be capable of visually discerning any difference between c_1 and c_2 (other than a difference in spatial position) if both were simultaneously presented for their visual inspection; i.e., neither could reidentify either of the two chairs. At t, then, Sandy and Chris are (still) in functionally identical states. They are, from Fodor's point of view, standing in the same cognitive-psychological relation (Perrian *acceptance*) to the same representation (a token of the mentalese equivalent of the type "That chair is an antique"). Hence, from the stand point of MS, they are in mental states of the same type.

Case B has two parts, each of which is concerned with one subject alone—let that one be Sandy. In B_1 we consider Sandy's internal functional state at two separate times, t and t'. As in case A. Sandy at t is in the same room, viewing c_1, uttering "That chair is an antique"; but at t' Sandy is in a qualitatively identical room, having a qualitatively identical visual experience while viewing c_2 and sincerely uttering the same words. Here, too, the functional states to be considered (Sandy at t, Sandy at t') are identical.

B_2 varies possible worlds, while holding t constant. We find Sandy at t in this world (w), exactly as described in A; and by way of contrast, at an alternative possible world w', which is exactly similar to w except for the fact that in w', Sandy is viewing c_2 at t. Again, Sandy is in the same mental state in both w and w', given the truth of MS.

There is a functional uniformity across all three pairs of belief scenarios: Chris and Sandy are in psychological states of the same type in A; and in B_1 and B_2, Sandy is in the same psychological state at t and t', and in w and w', respectively. There is a parallel *contrast* as well across the three cases. In A, B_1, and B_2 the first belief described has as its content the particular proposition $<x$ is an antique, $c_1>$, while the second has as content the proposition $<x$ is an antique, $c_2>$. I.e., in A, Sandy believes of c_1 that it is an antique and Chris, in virtue of being in a psychological state of the same type, believes of c_2 that *it* is an antique; in B_1, Sandy at t believes of c_1 that is is an antique, but at t' believes the same of c_2 and in B_2 Sandy has beliefs of these two different contents, not at different times, but in different worlds at the same time.

Taking S for Sandy and K for Chris, the three pairs of situations can be designated as follows:

A: (S, t, c_1, w); $(K, t, c_2, w$

B_1: (S, t, c_1, w); (S, t', c_2, w)

B_2: (S, t, c_1, w); (S, t, c_2, w').

Each ordered quadruple represents a *subject*, at a *time*, believing of an *object*, that it is an antique, at a *possible world*. (The use of possible worlds jargon is merely expedient here, as elsewhere in this work, and reflects no commitment to a possible-worlds analysis of alethic modalities.) Since the doctrine of psychologism in cognitive attitude theory implies at least that differences in complete sets of beliefs entail corresponding differences in complete sets of psychological states, we obtain absurdity in all three cases. In each pair, identity of psychological state types is *assumed* at the outset narrow state types, conformable to MS, of course. These three pairs of situations would be impossible if MS and psychologism were both true; we are accepting as relatively unproblematic the attributions of beliefs of the two *de re* propositions. As it is indeed perfectly possible for situation pairs of any one of these three sorts to occur, NPC is untenable.

Another, more advantageous way of specifying the position that I have been calling *psychologism* (in cognitive attitude theory) is available. As stated above, this is the position that cognitive attitudes simply *are* psychological states. The modified position, slightly weaker and perhaps somewhat clearer as well, is that one's psychological states fully determine all of one's cognitive attitudes, either singly or collectively. This version seems, prima facie, less hostile to MS . It is (we shall see, later, that it is not) difficult to imagine how mental representations could be purely formal if the original version were true: if my believing that the sky is blue just *is* my being in a psychological state of a certain type—i.e., my standing in a certain relation to a certain representation it is difficult not to construe the relation as that of believing (or accepting) and the *representation* as the proposition that the sky is blue (or a representation of that proposition). Hence it would be difficult to withhold semantic properties from mental representations in accordance with Fodorian MS. Because the revised version of psychologism is weaker, our denial of it will be a stronger statement than the denial of the original. Obviously the corresponding version of *narrow* psychologism (NPC) is equally untenable in light of our *de re* belief situation schemata above. Let us therefore adopt the new version as the official statement of psychologism.

This formulation itself suggests two basic alternative elaborations of psychologism. First of all, mental states may be seen as determining cognitive attitudes individually—i.e., each attitude may have one or more states associated with it, each of which necessitates the holding of the attitude. Alternatively, sets of attitudes may be viewed as determined by aggregations of states, or the subject's entire set of attitudes as determined only collectively by a sizable subset of his psychological states. These two orientations correspond to two basic alternatives open to the opponents of psychologism. Either 1) mental states taken singly, together with extramental facts, determine individual cognitive attitudes; or 2) groups of states, or larger states cutting across cognitive attitude boundaries, are needed together with nonmental reality in order fully to determine attitudes. The second alternative is just the denial of the assumption made in the first—viz., that states are tailor-made for attitudes and in the determination of the latter, individual states can actualize attitudes without supplementation by other *states*. By assuming total functional identity of Chris and Sandy at t in case A above, and similarly of Sandy-at-t and Sandy-at-t' in w (case B_1), and Sandy-at-w and Sandy-at-w' at t (case B_2), we need not deal with the two alternatives separately.

In sum, the pairs of scenarios have shown only that identity of functional state is compatible with diversity of (corresponding) attitude content, provided of course that the *de re* belief attributions are correctly made. Yet this amounts to the falsity of NPC, since functional identity, on MS, implies psychological identity, which, on psychologism, implies attitude identity.

Presupposed in the foregoing battery of thought experiments is a tolerance of *de re* attitudes about concrete particulars which is admittedly liberal by contemporary standards, but which could hardly he called radical or immoderate. From certain traditional perspectives, however, treating *de re* propositions as genuine contents of cognition on an equal footing with thoroughly general contents is seen as precarious heterodoxy. Not only are traditional *doctrines* challenged in this liberal orientation but violence is done to a body of cherished *intuitions* as well. Concrete objects, unlike Lockean ideas, are not diaphanous unities incorporable by the mind, i.e., digestible, without residue, in occurrent thought. They are therefore ill-fitted to serve as components of propositions that are thought (and thinkable) by us, according to the mainstream of empiricism. The intuitive revulsion felt toward an option countenancing a genus of thought contents characterized both by their irreducibility and by their inassimilability to experience solipsistically regarded, survives, at least vestigially, in much latter-day empiricistic sentiment. Manifestations in point include the majority of the endeavors to reduce *de re* to general belief—like those of Russell, Kaplan, Schiffer and Bach.

The devout descriptivist, one may guess, will not trust our attributions of *de re* content sufficiently to acquiesce in our conclusion in the thought experiments, that NPC is false. For him or her, the experiments should be assigned a quite different significance: they should be construed as a reductio ad absurdum of the position that *de re* content is both coherent and on a par with general content. Thus, it appears that there is a mutual antagonism between NPC and the possibility of irreducible *de re* belief; and that *which* of these doctrines one should repudiate depends upon one's alignment with respect to a more general theoretical division. In light of the discussion so far, either side of the fence would appear every bit as acceptable as the other.

De re belief might be done without if need be, to ensure the benefits accrued in the acceptance of the MS/psychologism combination. *De re* beliefs are not MS-style mental states, so either: i) beliefs in general are not MS-style mental states; or ii) *de re* beliefs are not really beliefs at all (though sense can be made of *de re* belief attributions).

If NPC could be refuted independently, the balance would be tipped entirely to side i). Attempts have been made in this direction, notably by Putnam and Burge, who have each argued strongly that general contents are not fully determined by internal (narrow) mental states either. The truth of this conclusion would clinch i), simply because there is no remotely tenable counterpart to option ii) above in the case of general belief.

Putnam's and Burge's arguments are centered upon thought experiments similar in design to our own. Their appeals to intuitions seem no less tenuous than ours: they fall short of achieving *knock-*

down arguments; yet the balance is clearly weighted in favor of i) without the use of any arm-twisting to elicit the "right" intuitions. Belief situations are introduced in pairs as with the examples of *de re* contents. The strategy is, as before, to hold constant the subject's total narrow mental state in both situations while varying a designated feature of the situation in such a way as to prompt the judgment that the contents believed differ between the two.

Putnam's argument concerns beliefs about natural kinds and explores the role played by the extension of a natural kind term in determining the content expressed by that term. In the basic thought experiment Putnam supposes the existence of another earth almost exactly like ours, quite distant from us. "Twin Earth," in fact, is a perfect duplicate of ours geographically, biologically? even psychologically—differing only in that the "water" of Twin Earth is not water (H_2O) but a different chemical compound *xyz* which nevertheless is indistinguishable from, (our) water except by chemical analysis. Let every man, woman, and child on Earth have an exact twin on Twin Earth whose history and all of whose (narrow) mental states match exactly with his or her own. English speakers on Twin Earth have a word 'water' which they use virtually as we do, but whereby they refer to *xyz* rather than H_2O. These inhabitants of Twin Earth have, just as we have, beliefs in the verbal articulation of which the term 'water' must be used. Can we say of these people that they have the concept *water* (our concept); that their beliefs about the liquid substance which is *xyz*, are really about water (H_2O)? Here are, strictly speaking, two separate questions, but there should be no doubt that if they do possess the concept (*our* concept), they also hold a set of beliefs about water. However it is (intuitively) clear that their beliefs expressible using the word 'water' are about the substance denoted by that word in the Twin Earth dialect of English, viz., *xyz*. Having never encountered water (i.e., H_2O), they lack a word for it. The concept corresponding to our concept of water is not a concept of *water* but rather of the other stuff. Thus although my Doppelgaenger on Twin Earth and I share exactly the same mental states (in the narrow sense), the content he expresses by uttering the sentence 'Oceans contain water' is different from the content I thereby express.

Some theoretical conclusions are extracted by Putnam from his experiment. Chief among these is the thesis that the actual extensions of natural kind terms play a causal role in the, determination of the meanings of such terms, and of propositional contents. This constitutes the development, in a certain direction, of what is commonly called the "Causal Theory of Reference." In the same vein, Putnam assimilates natural kind terms to indexical expressions: "Words like 'water' have an unnoticed indexical component: [the reference of] 'water' is stuff that bears a certain similarity relation to the water *around here*." He also accords them the rigidity of designation characteristic of proper names: "Water at another time or in another place or even in another possible world has to bear the relation same-L to *our* water *in order to be water*." (Here same-L means *same liquid*, a similarity relation that derives from certain theoretical generalizations in chemistry and physics.)

Another conclusion is that of the "division of linguistic labor": the delegating, to experts, by the rest of the linguistic community, of tasks of ascertaining the exact applications of predicates used by the whole of the community. An illustration of this principle is our use of the locution 'gold'. Very few of us are capable of deciding with certainty whether or not a piece of metal is gold. Few of us who are not metallurgists or chemists possess both infallible criteria of application of the expression and methods for determining whether these criteria are satisfied. Cognizance of a criterion—e.g., that something is pure gold if it is composed entirely of atoms with atomic number 79—without the knowledge how to conduct an empirical test for satisfaction of the criterion, is commonplace. On the other hand, those of us who fail to possess both a criterion and a way of implementing it are not thereby barred from holding propositional attitudes about gold (or water, etc.). The content gold serves as a component in many of my propositional contents, just as it does in propositional contents held by a chemist; yet I have no way of testing for satisfaction of the criterion.

(Must there exist in my linguistic community, past, present, or future, experts who are capable of determining with certainty whether or not something is gold, in order for *me* (a non-expert) to have the concept gold, use the term correctly, and hold propositional attitudes about gold? Putnam does not make this clear, although he intimates that the concept of water prior to 1750 might not be grounded in the expertise of chemists practicing in the subsequent maturity of their science. And if it is not grounded in that, then possibly it is not thus grounded at all. This is an issue to which I shall advert below.)

Burge's thought experiment proceeds by varying a different element of a belief situation, again keeping the subject's narrow psychological state constant. That element is *social* in character, and Burge's conclusions will be seen to cohere rather well with those of Putnam. Burge asks us to consider the case of a man who has come to believe (erroneously, of course) that he has arthritis in his thigh. In addition to this obviously false belief he has "a large number of attitudes commonly attributed with content clauses containing 'arthritis' in oblique occurrence," all of which are true. Among these are that "he has had arthritis for years, that his arthritis in his wrists and fingers is more painful than his arthritis in his ankles...." He reports to his doctor the suspicion that the arthritis has found its way into his thigh, and the doctor swiftly disabuses him of the thought, explaining that arthritis occurs only in the joints. Note that the erroneous belief was unproblematically one about arthritis: i.e., that the subject did not fail to have the concept *arthritis* merely by reason of his believing something impossible about the disease.

Step two in this experiment counterfactually varies the linguistic convention governing the use of 'arthritis', in such a way that the subject's suspicion that he has arthritis in the thigh is true. We are asked to consider an alternative possible state of affairs in which the disease called 'arthritis' comprises not just the usual inflammations of joints, but other rheumatoid ailments as well, in virtue of a wider communal acceptance of the term.

In the counterfactual state of affairs, the expression 'arthritis' does not mean—does not have as extension—the ailment arthritis but some other ailment. (For arthritis is necessarily an affliction of the joints, whereas the counterfactual extension of the term occurs not only in joints, but also in the limbs themselves.) The patient then has, not the notion of *arthritis* (*our* notion), but another notion. Burge argues that

> counterpart expressions in content clauses that are actually and counterfactually ascribable are not even extensionally equivalent. However we describe the patient's attitudes in the counterfactual situation, it will not be with a term or phrase extensionally equivalent with 'arthritis'. So the patient's counterfactual attitude contents differ from his actual ones. (p.79)

We are led to conclude (as with Putnam's thought experiment) that not even a subject's *total* narrow psychological state is sufficient for his holding of cognitive attitudes whose contents incorporate any of a wide range of general nations. The very state-type that psychologically underlies a certain belief about arthritis in actuality, may underlie a belief about some other disease in an alternative world, one in which linguistic conventions differ only slightly from our own.

Putnam's and Burge's thought experiments, together with our own arguments involving *de re* beliefs, should be deemed sufficient to lay NPC to rest. They fail, however, to point out which of its two conjuncts is defective (conceivably both are false, but it is atypical to reject both). The "individualism" against which Burge argues is, in its strongest form, indistinguishable from NPC. At least two weaker forms of individualism are left unscathed by the thought experiments and their immediate conclusions: one is MS itself—a psychological individualism; the other is a weak epistemic, or cognitive, individualism. Both are compatible with the denial of psychologism in content theory. The former (MS) will be defended on grounds of theoretical economy; it being true, psychologist must be renounced to avoid the implication of NPC. The latter, as a methodological guideline, will then be adopted in the interests of preserving our evaluative practice of cognitive attitude ascription.

So far, three different versions of MS have been stated: first the pre-theoretical version, viz. that psychological states are thoroughly internal to the subject; then Putnam's definition; and Fodor's conception of MS as the conjunction of the representational theory of mind and a formality condition. But now, for the purpose of defending the thesis, a definitive version of methodological solipsism is needed. Let us, in refining the position, adhere to Putnam's definition, simply making modifications where necessary—in order to conform the final definition to the main conclusion of his Twin Earth thought experiment. One advantage of Putnan's version is that it more closely resembles the notion of solipsism per se, the idea that one is alone in the world, or is all that exists. Following Putnam in this fashion will also have the advantage of avoiding commitment to Fodor's (somewhat vaguely articulated) representationalism.

In Putnam's definition there is an ambiguity in the scope of 'any' the resolution of which will lead to a more perspicuous formulation. On the wide reading, MS is the assumption that

A)   For a psychological state of type T, there is not any individual x other than the subject S, such that S's being in T presupposes the existence of x.

Alternatively, giving 'any' narrow scope, MS is the assumption that

B)   For a psychological state of type T, it is not the case that a subject S's being in T presupposes that there exists anything at all besides S himself.

On the wide reading, a subject's being in a psychological state merely fails to entail the existence of any specific individual. Thus, for example, if A) were true, it could nevertheless be the case that being in a certain psychological state entailed the existence of philosophers, yet it is impossible that being in any state could entail the existence of W.V. Quine. On the other hand, the B) reading prohibits being in a psychological state from presupposing the existence of anything. Thus every state must be such that a subject's being in it is compatible with the subject's being the only existent entity.

Individuals may be viewed as semantic contents of cognition, just as general propositional components are. Certainly if a subject holds a cognitive attitude about a concrete individual, that individual must exist.[1] But similarly, if Putnam is right about this (and I believe he is), there are certain general propositional components whose instantiation in the real world is implied by their occurring in contents of cognitive attitudes. The most familiar of these are the natural kind concepts. Thus, for me actually to hold a belief about water, some water must exist, or must have existed in the past, in order to initiate a causal chain grounding my grasp of the concept.

Narrow—i.e., methodologically solipsistic—psychological states that underlie cognitive attitudes, however, carry no such implications: neither implications of the existence of *some individual or other*, of a specified kind, (e.g., bodies of water), nor of the existence of some particular individual of that kind (e.g., Lake Tahoe). The best way to rule out all such implications seems to be to choose reading B)—the narrow construal of Putnam's definition—over reading A). Note that, if a system of state types could be "narrow" just by making no presuppositions as to which individuals distinct from the subject there must be—as per A)—then of course the holding of all the familiar cognitive attitudes about water would qualify as a corpus of "narrow" psychological states. This would contradict the central result of the thought experiment. Mental states of the category allowed by A) would be recognized by a typical adherent of the descriptivism mentioned earlier. They would not be characterized by any such theorist as "narrow", however, as there would be (for him) no coherent conception of *wide* psychological states by way of contrast, *de re* cognition being renounced as incoherent. The descriptivist would reject the B) version as unduly limit-

---

1. Provided that the attitude is truly de re: we shall deal briefly with fictional characters, etc. later.

ing our powers of cognition; hence, on psychologistic grounds, unduly restrictive of *mental* power or capacity. The primary virtue of reading B) is, of course, that on this version the possibility will be excluded, that any propositional content of the sort whose grasp requires a causal connection will be implicated in the ascription of any psychological state.

A more appropriate approach than either A) or B) would seem to be that of attempting to express the doctrine of MS by direct reference to the absence, on the part of psychological states, of any implication of propositional content. Fodor's formality condition evidently supports the absence of any content-implication: mental states and their constituents are to be intrinsically uninterpreted; they are not accompanied by any semantic content. Underdetermination of semantic contents of thought by psychological states is the essence of this position. Hence let us call the following thesis UD, the Undetermination Thesis

UD   A subject's being in a psychological state of type T fails to imply, of any propositional component c (either particular or general) that c is grasped by the subject or that any proposition containing c is a content of a propositional attitude held by the subject

Framed in these terms, as the underdetermination (i.e., non-determination) of contents of thought by psychological states, MS would be most obviously inimical to the doctrine of psychologism, which amounts to strict determination of contents by psychological states.

How convenient it would be if MS could be defended in this guise: all psychological states and combinations thereof portrayed as underdetermining semantic contents! However there are apparent exceptions that tell strongly against this version of MS. The most salient of these are propositions that are simple logical truths. For example, the law of modus ponens: that if P is true and P implies G, then Q is true. In order to grasp, and to believe, this proposition, how could it be necessary for a subject to be in causal contact with any special properties or relations in the physical world? Other a priori truths appear to require no causal connection for their cognitive grasp, such as a proposition about causation itself: that if events of type *B* are caused only by events of type *A*, and if an event of type *B* has occurred, then an event of type *A* has occurred. These and other propositions might all be thought to have components that are fully determined by appropriate (combinations of) mental state types—thus controverting the underdetermination thesis. Let us call any such propositions and their components "inner conceptual contents." It is imperative that we at least *allow for the possibility* that inner conceptual contents may exist: that certain general propositional components may require no causal warrant, being determined by single psychological states, or by configurations of such states.

Kent Bach suggests, contra Fodor, that mental representations may have "conceptual properties" very like Fregean *Sinne*, that figure in their individuation. This amounts to the claim that the formality condition is excessively strong. Bach assumes, first, that some semantically identical pairs of sentences such as 'Blood is thicker than water' and 'Water is thinner than blood' are such that the same psychological state underlies the acceptance of both; and second, that the respective mental representations are formally distinct. Yet the formality condition implies that a psychological state type determines a subject's relation to a certain representation, and not just conversely. The variety of MS that eschews the formality condition Bach calls Conceptual Methodological Solipsism (CMS), as distinguished from Formal MS (FMS).

The questions that must now arise are: What are these conceptual properties, and what has CMS to do with inner conceptual contents? One possible reply to both questions involves identifying the conceptual properties with the inner contents, and stipulating that at least some of these properties (contents) are Fregean Sinne, and that all are *like* Sinne, remembering of course that not all Sinne can be *inner* conceptual contents (case in point: the semantic content WATER). A similar answer, with no commitment to the Fregean ontology, would merely substitute 'cognitive contents' for Sinne. (A word or two on terminology is long overdue at this point. *Cognitive* contents include, but are not restricted to, propositions and propositional components. *Conceptual* contents are general cognitive contents, so naturally include general propositional components, and propositions compounded solely of these (i.e., thoroughly general propositions. *Semantic* contents are just cognitive contents, no more and no less.)

CMS is an interesting thesis for two principal reasons. The first is that it must emphasize that some conceptual contents are indeed *inner*, i.e., fully determined by (constellations of) narrow psychological states. Even if this were to turn out to be false, it would not detract from the argument for MS that follows; we would merely (re) adopt the stronger version of MS (viz., UD). The second reason is that some contents, or conceptual properties, on this theory, are not exactly propositional components. Let us, just in passing, examine the conceptual property characterizing the semantic identity of the proposition expressed by the two sentences 'Blood is thicker than water' and 'Water is thinner than blood. Note, first of all, that the concepts of blood, water, thicker than, and thinner than, are not themselves inner conceptual contents—at least the concepts of blood and water surely are not, as they are natural kind concepts. Yet there is a certain piece of semantic knowledge, that *thinner than* and *thicker than* bear a reciprocal relationship to one another. This bit of knowledge constrains the use, in language and thought, of the two concepts. The relationship itself either is, or is intimately connected with, the conceptual property that (in Fodorian parlance) contributes to the individuation of the relevant mental representation. Whether it is identical with that property, or just inseparably connected with it, is not especially crucial for our purposes. The task at hand is to arrive at a characterization of MS that is compatible with the truth of CMS, as the latter appears likely to be true, if matters are viewed from the representationalist standpoint.

Returning, then, to the problem of formulating MS with a view to all the foregoing considerations, it is useful to look back at interpretation B) of Putnam's definition. As it turns out, this version of MS would be perfectly satisfactory except for the desirability of framing the thesis in terms of non-implication of content (general and particular propositional contents) by psychological states. So our formulation should be equivalent to B), but framed in these terms. MS in its definitive form must depend, to an extent, upon a theory of content. As the theory of content itself will depend somewhat upon a methodologically solipsistic psychology, there is apparently no way to avoid a certain circularity. But since the circle is a rather "big circle", the circularity is relatively innocuous. I shall label the definition itself MS

MS A psychological theory conforms to methodological solipsism iff it allows no psychological state type (or configuration of state types) whose ascription, per se, to a subject entails the subject's grasp of any cognitive content, the grasp of which requires a definite causal link with the outside world.

Let us unpack the definition: MS is the thesis that all psychological states are narrow, and the definition circumscribes the property of narrowness, by reference to absence of certain content implications. As for particular (de re) contents, none are determined by psychological states, as all involve the causal connection between the subject and a concrete individual. Neither are any general contents determined, for whose grasp the causal connection with the physical world is necessary. The choice is clearly left open to adherents of MS, either to espouse something like CMS—i.e., to acknowledge inner conceptual contents—or not. Thus MS is still cast as an underdetermination thesis, yet one somewhat weaker than UD.

The basic argument to establish MS is quite simple. It is in fact a reductio ad absurdum of psychologism. This will in actuality yield something slightly weaker still than the thesis reflected in the definition MS—viz., the thesis that psychological state does not always and necessarily determine cognitive content. Yet since the design of the argument is generalizable to all the relevant sorts of cases, it should be easy to recognize that it does indeed support the truth of MS.

We refute psychologism by first assuming it true: assuming that psychological state is thoroughly determinative of all content. In other words, the total psychological state, or set of states, that a subject is in at a single time, must determine exactly one total set of beliefs held by that subject at that time. If this is so, then any difference in content (of belief, say) in an individual subject must be underlain by a difference in psychological state. A difference in psychological state must, in turn, be accompanied by a corresponding, underlying difference in physiological state. Thus any difference in content implies a difference in physiological state. But we may see from a thought experiment similar to those conducted above, that a subject may be in a single total physiological state in two different possible worlds, and yet hold different beliefs in those worlds. And this, of course, is inconsistent with the foregoing assumptions.

As the aforestated implication relation between physiological states and psychological states is essential to this argument, the nature of the relation must be considered, and the acceptance of it justified. Although strictly speaking, it is the total physiological state of the subject that is important here, what is of primary interest is the total neurological or brain state. I am holding that, because psychological causation of behavior must be supervenient upon physiological causation of behavior, any total physiological state may underlie only one total psychological state. This is to say that a person's total psychological state is fully determined, at any given time, by the total physiological (neurological) state the person is in at that time. This is not a causal, but rather a logical determination, even though the laws (bridge laws) that prescribe just how the physiological determines the psychological are not logical truths.

Each subject, at any given time, is in a large number of psychological states, as well as a large number of physiological states. There is, in each category, the *total* state, which comprises a multitude of less comprehensive states at various levels. Suppose there is a type of psychological state that is "seeming to see a red rose." If I am presently in a state of that type, my being so is encompassed by my being in a *total* psychological state, which also includes larger, more comprehensive states than that of seeming to see a red rose. So we may speak of a total state, and of substates at different levels of comprehensiveness, in both the psychological and the physiological realms.

Psychological explanation is, and must be, a form of causal explanation—explanation of behavior in the light of current psychological states and occurrent stimuli. Any change across time or difference across possible worlds, of any magnitude, in a subject's psychological state must reflect a difference in the subject's *propensity* to produce behavior even if that difference in propensity would effect no difference in the actual behavior produced. This must be the case, in order for the psychological theory postulating the pertinent assortment of state types, to remain faithful to its sole purpose of causal explanation of behavior. If a difference in psychological state type makes no difference even in the subject's disposition to behave, then there can be no genuine psychological distinction between the two types of states: in a legitimate psychological theory, supposing a variation, across possible worlds, of a subject's total psychological state *must* involve varying the subject's total propensity to behave.

However, no matter how numerous and multifarious the set of psychological states, processes, and laws may become, it is doubtful that even the best psychological theory could ever attain the degree of explanatory adequacy expected of physiological theory. It is on the physiological level that the "real" causation of behavior occurs. I.e., causation requires not just a temporal, but also a thoroughly physical, spatial dimension, in which to effect change. The spatial dimension is not present in the psychological realm; hence the supervenience of the psychological upon the physiological. There can be no doubt, then, that every difference in propensity to behave must be underlain, not only by a difference in psychological state, but by a difference in physiological state as well. Thus, this should be sufficient to establish that a difference in psychological state must be accompanied by a difference in physiological state.

All that remains in the defense of MS, then, is to sketch the physiology-invariant thought experiment. Let the doxastic subject, Martha, view an antique table in the actual world w_0 at a given time t. We may consider another possible world, w_1, extremely close to the actual world, in which all that is different is the identity of the table, and the fact that it is not an antique, but rather a facsimile. The scenario in this experiment is similar to that of a previous one, but here we shall focus upon the identity of Martha's total physiological state, and in particular, her total neurological state, between the actual world w_0 and the near alternative w_1. Her physiological state remains the same, as it is only the identity of the table that changes in the transition from w_0 to w_1. Yet the subject's belief at $<w_0, t>$ is different in content from her belief at $<w_1, t>$. So, to complete the reductio argument, we may conclude that a subject may hold different total sets of beliefs in two possible worlds at a given time, while yet being in exactly the same physiological state in both those worlds at that time.

Part II

Epistemic Values and
Epistemic Stratification

1

Thus psychology is enjoined *not* to include cognitive content in its principles of identification or psychological states. The concern of the present chapter will be a characterization of cognitive psychology's relation to the theory of cognitive content. This project will include a more general exploration of the realm of the mental, briefly in its usual common-sense or naive conception, and in the theoretical conception that results from our endeavor to disentangle and clarify the various strands which appear to be present in the naive picture. Ultimately, the study and articulation of the several phases and aspects of mentality and cognition will issue in the development and imposition of necessary conditions upon the entertaining (and believing, etc.) of general and particular thoughts, respectively.

Pursuant to the establishment of MS and the corresponding renunciation of psychologism, work in content theory will assume a general direction of inquiry into the character of trans-psychological ingredients in the grasp of contents (i.e., constituents of the act of grasping other than psychological states themselves). As an initial step in that direction, it should be acknowledged that a minimum constituent feature is that of a situation or state of affairs in the extramental world. Note that this is reminiscent of a certain necessary condition on knowledge that has a propositional object: viz., that the proposition be true. Indeed, the existence of a particular individual, or the instantiation of a property or relation in the actual world, is requisite to the grasping of propositional components of these respective categories, in very much the same way that the truth of a proposition is requisite to the knowledge of that proposition. These two ways in which the (extramental) world enters into two species of cognitive phenomena, neither of which is a purely psychological phenomenon, are clearly comparable. (Note that existence and instantiation have as linguistic counterparts singular and divided reference.) Also comparable are the causal requirement on knowledge, generally accepted since the publication of Gettier's famous article, and the requirement of a causal link (of a certain sort) in the grasping of empirical contents. In the justification of a belief, the subject's information must have been appropriately caused, if knowledge of the proposition at hand can be truly attributed to him. And similarly, as is emphasized in Putnam's paper and much of the discussion it has engendered, the grasp of a propositional component involves the correct causation, *by* the component, of the underlying state of mind. (For example, my grasp of the meaning of 'water', to be legitimate, must have been caused, in a special way, by water itself.)

Enough of a parallel between theory of content and theory of knowledge seems to be emerging, that serious consideration should be given to an assimilation of the two disciplines, or subsumption of both under a third. I shall argue that, in fact, content theory is a subtheory of epistemology, and that an understanding of cognitive content and its determination is essential to an understanding of how we know, and what we are capable of knowing. So far, the parallel consists in two pairs of requirements on grasping and knowing—one pair pertaining to the character of the (extramental) world itself, the other to the causal pedigree of the relevant parcel of information. The causal requirement is not, in epistemology, strictly coextensive with the requirement of justification, but rather is concerned with relative etiologies of the relata of justification. Let us defer for now the question whether the notion of justification itself has a counterpart in the theory of content, and inquire below, whether the causal requirement in content theory fits into any such scheme as it does in theory of knowledge.

The traditional conception of knowledge as justified true belief engenders a fundamental stratification of the epistemological domain. On the first level is belief simpliciter, which by itself fails to constitute knowledge—as Plato famously admonishes in the *Theatetus*. Next, on the same level, are the realm of justified belief—which may have either true or false contents, and the realm of belief of true contents—which may be either justified or unjustified. These realms overlap, occupying that stratum intermediate between belief and genuine knowledge. Knowledge itself is on the top level, the intersection of other domains. This is but an oversimplified sketch of the stratification in theory of knowledge. Further structural complexities must accompany the causal requirement, but a description of this additional structure awaits an adequately clear and precise statement of that requirement. Such a formulation will be worthwhile to pursue below. At this stage, it is enough to recognize the power and utility of the stratification paradigm.

A natural move, warranted by the plausible hypothesis that content theory is a part or a species of epistemology, is now to extend that paradigm to the sphere of content theory. Thus one level would comprise psychological states alone; one would comprise psychological states which, *were* they appropriately caused, *would* properly underlie the grasp of some legitimate (i.e., existent or instantiated) content. (At the latter level might also be states which, although proceeding causally from actual propositional components in the world, are simply of the wrong *form* to support grasp of those components.) Furthermore, there must be the level of genuine grasp of complete propositions, and their sub-propositional components. This is, again, an oversimplification. Content theory, in its detailed development, will exhibit more than three strata, as well as a host of principles that bind the various levels together.

Not only does it behoove us to postulate a stratification in content theory which closely resembles that found in theory of knowledge: the further step, of superposing the one family of strata directly above the other, in one grand epistemological hierarchy, is virtually unavoidable. The inducement is of course continuity. In the content theoretical hierarchy, the grasp of propositional contents and their components is the top level, and is but a single step away from the level of belief, the latter being typically located at the base of the theory-of-knowledge hierarchy. The grasp of a proposition is an ingredient in its belief, just as belief is an ingredient in justified belief and also in knowledge. The inclusion, in a larger epistemological theory, of a content theory possessing several strata, is a strongly anti-psychologistic maneuver: it is immaterial whether a psychologistic theory of knowledge takes grasping of content (cognitive/semantic competence) or *believing* as the ground floor, the lowest level in its stratified theory of knowledge If a theory of knowledge is indeed psychologistic, both believing and grasping will be written off by it as psychological phenomena—sharing a single level that is, epistemologically speaking, unstratified, and as such, insusceptible of epistemological analysis. The effect will then be an obfuscation of the levels intervening between the purely psychological and the stratum of cognitive grasp—thus depriving the theory, in this region, of the benefit of illumination of *normative* principles of epistemology. (More will be said of these normative principles and their role.)

The failure to recognize a region intermediate between psychological states and cognitive grasp is symptomatic of the common, yet perhaps largely inadvertent, inclination to conflate psychological states and content states. The naive conception of the mental contains folk psychology, which is learned early in life, during the very process of language acquisition. So along with pains, itches, and sensations of red, we come to classify beliefs, doubts, desires, seekings, and so on, as psychological states from the very start. There are at least two other important strands in our naive, or common-sense conception of the mental. These, embraced together with folk psychology, give rise to the conflation, which, because the common-sense conception is deeply ingrained, is difficult to resist.

One of the strands is the conception of the mental realm as the medium of causation of behavior. This fits together neatly with the notion that psychology is an empirical science, i.e., is a subject-matter to be studied empirically since causal principles are, in general, the concern of empirical inquiry. On this view of psychology, all of the types of mental states, properties, and processes mentioned in a psychological theory will have been posited for the purpose of playing certain roles in nomological generalizations about behavior. Since the observable quantities in such a science must initially refrain from implying anything about the internal structures posited, the theory must use descriptions of these quantities that are neutral with respect to the nature of those structures. Behavior, taken under a neutral (i.e., non-intentional) description must be restricted to motion or action of an individual, and input, to be described neutrally, must be framed merely as sensory reception. Behavioristic generalizations, nomologically associating patterns of input with patterns of output, will always prove inadequate; hence the need for a *medium* that is at least partially autonomous.

The third major strand is phenomenological. The chief characteristics of mentality from this perspective are those of intentionality—mainly consciousness, introspectability, and object-directness. Other properties included by Brentano and Husserl, and other writers, in the idea of intentionality might also enter into this conception. It is arguable that the phenomenological realm contains inner conceptual contents of the sort discussed in the previous section.

Whether the second and third strands turn out to be compatible in their respective technical elaborations is not important (although they are consistent as I have rather vaguely stated them). Phenomenology may turn out, in the light of empirical and philosophical research, to be obviously devoid of viability. What is important is that neither is compatible with folk psychology. The states of folk psychology may be classified as either cognitive or non-cognitive. The non-cognitive states (being in pain, seeming to see blue, etc.) are also phenomenological states, but the cognitive states, viz., propositional attitudes, are not. They cannot be, strictly speaking, phenomenological states, because their contents, being denizens of the extramental world, are not introspectible.

The second (empirical) strand is incompatible with folk psychology for a different reason: the necessity of imposing MS on any scientific psychological theory. In empirical psychology, the taxonomy of states must be narrow, i.e., methodologically solipsistic, thus prohibiting folk-psychological states, which are intrinsically wide, from being genuine psychological states. With regard to these three strands, then, the options seem to be either to claim that folk psychology deals with the truly psychological, and that empirical psychology and phenomenology do not; or to contend that the second and third strands do pertain to the realm of the mental, and that folk psychology is not really psychology, but rather something else. I shall choose the latter course, but shall provide qualifications that will vindicate the practice of folk psychology as an explanatory theory.

Despite Jerry Fodor's professed commitment to MS, he flirts with a doctrine that he designates "naturalism," that either allows, or insists upon, a wide taxonomy of mental states depending on the strength of the version held. I elect to call the position "quasi-naturalism," for, in neither of its versions is it as extremely naturalistic as Quine's brand of naturalized epistemology (as we shall see presently). There are two basic grades of quasi-naturalism. *Pure* quasi-naturalism, or QN_1, is the view that only a wide taxonomy of mental states is called for in cognitive psychology; and QN_2, or *mixed* quasi-naturalism, is the view that both wide and narrow taxonomies are possible and useful. The latter—mixed—species amounts to the doctrine that there should ideally be two rather different bodies of psychological theory. Fodor endorses this impure form, but somewhat hesitantly. He believes that, although it is imperative that we acknowledge a narrow (MS) taxonomy, there may or may not be a legitimate place in cognitive psychology for a theory incorporating a wide taxonomy as well, according as a wide (sub-) theory is practically attainable or not. Whether there is indeed such a place, he holds, is thus contingent on future results of empirical research along the lines of semantic connections between mind and world.

The pure form, QN_1, is antithetical to MS, and should be dismissed on the grounds of our acceptance of MS. QN_2, however, is an interesting and attractive thesis, with much to recommend it, even though ultimately it, too, is contrary to the spirit and letter of MS. Why might we be inclined to allow a system of wide psychological state types in addition to the methodologically solipsistic system? Apparently to fill an important explanatory need—the need to couch explanandum and explanans alike in wide, propositional attitudinal terms. I shall not deny the need, but only the assumption that a wide psychological taxonomy is indispensable to its satisfaction.

Demands for explanations of behavior typically describe the behavior as intentional action rather than as mere bodily notion, neutrally conceived. Thus we will typically inquire, "Why did James Bond shoot the Soviet agent?" instead of "Why did Bond contract the muscles in the second and third segments of his right index finger?"—even though the latter movement is precisely the physical act whereby he discharges the gun, felling the Soviet agent. The answer to such a question, too, is almost invariably framed in intentional terms rather than as descriptions of narrow mental states, sensory-receptive episodes, and conditional laws whose consequents are descriptions of bodily movements. The reply, "Because Bond saw the Russian spy reaching for a weapon, and believed that he (Russian) would surely kill him (Bond) first if he succeeded in laying hands on that weapon," is intelligible to us, and seems a satisfactory explanation. Its narrow counterpart, however, would be incomprehensible, save to someone who knew *which* complex sensory-receptive pattern constituted Bond's seeing the enemy agent grab for the weapon; who knew which mental state underlay Bond's belief; and who possessed a considerable quantity of background knowledge about the physical situation in which the actions transpired. It is not even clear what the description of Bond's psychological state would look like, as a mature theory of cognitive psychology still lies somewhere in the future. Yet even upon the development of an explanatorily adequate narrow system, it is unlikely that everyday explanations of persons' actions will cease to be wide (folk-psychological) explanations. There are certain *pragmatic needs* that attend a request for an explanation of behavior, and most of these are usually met by the traditional wide explanations. Folk-psychological explanations are legitimate, and often accurate, so far as they go. I am maintaining, however, that they are not themselves psychological explanations in the strict sense, but that they rely on there being, at least in principle, a system, of true nomological generalizations whose ideology conforms to the dictates of MS.

In order to depict, schematically, what actually happens in a folk-psychological explanation of a piece of behavior—including the mechanism of the tacit appeal to a highly developed narrow theory—a number of different elements of the explanatory scenario must be identified. I'll give them convenient abbreviations, as follows. The *wide output* (*WO*) is the explanandum, the bit of behavior to be explained, described in folk-psychological idiom, usually as an intentional action. The *wide input* (*WI*) is the folk-psychological description of sensory input relevant to (as, e.g., precipitating) the behavior. This is, if mentioned at all, usually in the form of reports of perception, not mere *reception*. The object of perception may be an individual (e.g., Jimmy Carter), a scene (Jimmy wearing cowboy boots, Jimmy shaking hands with Willie Nelson), a proposition (that Jimmy has just hit a home run)—in general, any object or complement of a perceptual verb. (This variability presents some problems for a detailed expositions that I shall not undertake to solve here.) Some sensory information received by the subject/ agent during the interval in question, may be implicit in the pragmatics of the explanatory dialogue, yet should be included explicitly in a complete specification of *WI*.

There are *wide* psychological *states* (*WS*), primarily propositional attitudes, of the subject/agent, stated explicitly, virtually without exception in the course of an explanation. This element is also frequently partly tacit, however: more wide states are included in WS than are explicitly attributed; although never is anything like a total inventory of wide psychological states provided.

The First element (*WO*) is the explanandum, the second (*WI*) and third (*WS*) together constitute the explanans, of a folk-psychological explanation. But there is also a *situational context* (*SC*) of the behavior, which must be drawn upon in certain implicational relationships behind the scenes of the explanatory dialogue. This *SC* is composed of the actual physical situation in which the behavior takes place: a region of space-time together with all the objects and events occurring therein. It may also contain a moderate amount of background information, pragmatically understood by, and accessible to, the parties of the dialogue (i.e., the party requesting, and the party providing, the explanation). This context will be needed to get from narrow states to wide states (and for little else); with this in mind, we may leave its definition vague.

Since the folk-psychological explanation "rides piggyback" on a counterpart *narrow* explanation, which carries the nomological burden, we need three corresponding narrow elements. First, a *total narrow state* (*TN*), which of course will not have to be specified in the course of any explanation. Secondly, a narrow, or neutral, description of the *input* (*NI*): this will just be sensory reception underlying *WI*. Thirdly, we require a *narrow* (again, neutral) description of the *behavior* (*NB*), the explanandum of the narrow explanation. Finally, just for the sake of completeness, we might desire a designation for the *new* total narrow state (*NN*) produced by the action of the input (*NI*) and behavioral output (*NB*) upon the initial total narrow state (*TN*)

We are prepared, at this point, to outline the relations among the various elements. Of the relations, there are three classes: logical, causal, and pseudo-causal. The logical relations hold between

the narrow elements and their respective wide counterparts, in virtue of generalizations I shall call "bridge laws," even though I don't
wish to imply that anything like a true reduction is occurring here.
The bridge laws in this scheme are essentially laws of content determination (and other laws similar in function), and thus we may
expect them to be of some appreciable complexity, and their exact
character to be a matter of a fair amount of contoversy. Their pecu-
liarity may be emphasized by pointing out that their nature is sub-
stantially *normative*—and this is a central tenet in my theory of
cognition, to whose defense I shall advert shortly. The roles of the
bridge laws in the folk-explanatory scheme can be stated very con-
cisely, despite the mystery in which their actual substance must
remain temporarily enveloped: i) the conjunction of *NB* and *SC*
implies *WO*; ii) the conjunction of *NI* and *SC* implies *WI;* and iii)
the conjunction of *TN* and *SC* implies *WS*. In short, the wide elements, both explicit and pragmatically implicit, in the explanatory
dialogue, are entailed through the bridge laws, by the corresponding narrow elements together with the situational context. We
might in fact sharpen the notion of *SC* by stipulating that it includes
everything in the extramental world that is needed in the determination of the contents at issue.

The causal relations in question hold only in the realm of methodologically solipsistic psychology. At the hub of the whole
endeavor is the presupposition that there is a system of nomological
generalizations, a theory of cognitive psychology, conforming to
MS. It is certainly unobjectionable that this supposition take the
form that the theory exists only in principle, not yet having been
developed in actual practice. Any sensory input together with a consequent behavioral output must have narrow descriptions that allow
an explanatory link making reference to the "properly" psychological laws of causation of behavior—i.e., the methodologically solipsistic ones. These laws are conditional in form: *if* the subject is in
the total narrow state TN_{-i} and receives input NI_{-i}, *then* he will perform behavior NB_i and enter the new total state NN_{-i} (or TN_{-i+1}). It

is easy to imagine instances of this schema in which the NI_i element or the NB_i element is empty: i.e., in which no new input is received or no new behavior is produced.

The pseudo-causal relations hold between *WS* and *WI* on the one hand, and *WO* on the other. Folk-psychological explanations are of such a form that it is proper to say that *this instance* of *WO*-i; that is, that a *token* of the relevant *WS* type conjoined with a *token* of the relevant *WI* type has resulted in a token of the relevant *WO* type. But causal laws in a bona fide theory of cognitive psychology cannot be formulated in terms of wide state-type's (or input-types or output-types). None of these types are either empirical quantities or allowable empirical constructs: as adumbrated above, propositional attitudes and cognitive contents have an inescapable normative, evaluative dimension, and wide state types are *defined by* the attitudes and contents associated with them: i.e., some normative elements are essential to their character, rendering them unsuitable as empirical constructs. This is not to say that lawlike, counterfactual-supporting generalizations could not be built up using wide-state properties. It is in fact likely that they could; but they would fail to qualify as psychological *laws*—not only by reason of the normative considerations, but by reason of considerations of utility as well. The pragmatic needs of explanation that would be served by adopting such laws *in addition* to the laws of a narrow theory—as per QN$_2$—can be served *without* treating them as laws, by keeping folk-explanation on a pseudo-causal level, delegating all the nomological duties to the narrow theory. Furthermore, QN$_2$ would violate the requirement of theoretical economy in still another way: to each total narrow psychological state there corresponds a multitude of total wide state types. Given a total narrow state, one need only significantly vary the possible world in order to produce an alteration in the totality of wide state types that is underlain by the narrow configuration. This implies that a psychological theory can get by with a far smaller set of narrow state types than the set of wide state types that would be needed.

Quasi-naturalism is a form of naturalism, inasmuch as it implies that cognitive contents occur as properties in an empirical science. It is nevertheless not a fully naturalistic doctrine because it does not imply that epistemology or the general theory of cognition call be thoroughly managed by—i.e., absorbed into—an empirical science. By contrast, Quine's radical version of naturalism does include this stronger claim. He contends that epistemology should be subsumed by psychology, and should be pursued *as* psychology, solely within the confines of the latter. Quine also insists upon a behavioristic psychology, eschewing the representational, and avoiding reference to intensional notions, such as propositions or properties, in his epistemology. Clad in generic garb, naturalism is the thesis that cognitive phenomena such as grasp, belief, justification, knowledge, can be accorded an adequate explication and development within empirical psychology, *qua* psychological phenomena. (Note that the appellation 'cognitive psychology' can be seriously misleading for a venture in which these *cognitive* phenomena will not turn out to be properly psychological concerns, unless it is made clear that cognitive psychology is the study of those psychological structures that support or realize ("underlie") cognitive phenomena.)

Apart from the arguments for MS, there is a fairly straightforward reputation of cognitive naturalism in all its forms. Let us attend just to the Fodorian (quasi) and Quinean forms: the thesis that cognitive contents are psychological states (i.e., that ascription of content is a wholly empirical matter), and the view that epistemological laws are psychological (i.e., empirically discoverable), respectively. I shall attempt first to establish that the criteria for *knowing* a proposition are not empirical this of course carries the implication that ascriptions of knowledge cannot be arrived at from data and general principles that are totally empirical. Then, having disposed of knowledge, we may turn to the grasp of components of cognitive contents.

In attributing to a subject the knowledge of some proposition, we make a descriptive statement that certain information is possessed by that subject: we predicate of her a familiarity with a given part of the world—whether this be a particular fact or a general principle. Such a familiarity is tantamount to an ability of sorts, the ability to "get around" in the pertinent region of the world—an ability that has a definite instrumental value; *adaptive* value if not fundamental *survival* value. The ability affords her a (potential) power to order her attitudes and actions in a way beneficial to herself and others. Knowing, of a certain variety of mushroom, that it is invariably lethal if ingested, for instance, motivates her to avoid picking and eating specimens of that variety, and motivates her to caution others against doing so.

Yet the instrumental value of knowledge does not differ from the instrumental value of true belief! Holding a true belief, *with or without* sufficient justification, affords the subject the same adaptive ability, the ability to get along successfully in a range of situations. Not only has knowledge no instrumental advantage over true belief; neither has the *attribution of* knowledge any *explanatory* advantage over attribution of belief simpliciter. Suppose that in a folk-psychological explanation of a bit of behavior, part of the explanans (specifically part of the *WS*), is the subject's knowledge that this species of mushroom is poisonous. Now consider an alternative explanans, which differs from the original only in that, instead of knowledge that it is poisonous, mere belief is attributed. Comparing the two alternatives, it is obvious that they do not differ in explanatory power, since the explanatory weight is being borne, not by the *WS*, but by the narrow psychological state, which is one and the same state underlying both the belief that *P* and the knowledge that *P* (indeed it underlies the knowledge precisely because it underlies the belief).

What, then, is the point of attributing knowledge? The answer must again invoke the sphere of value; but here we discern a difference between knowledge and belief: a difference in *intrinsic* value. Knowledge carries an intrinsic value that any belief which falls short of knowledge—either by way of false content, or through absence of adequate justification—fails to have. Knowledge is a virtue that mere belief is not. Wherein lies that virtue? One might characterize it as the intrinsic good of having internalized or assimilated definite parts of the extramental world. It is to be anticipated, then, that a general or schematic *criterion* of knowledge, a stipulation of kinds and degrees of conditions requisite to knowledge, must subserve the intrinsic value that distinguishes knowledge from belief. In other words, whatever conditions are settled on as jointly necessary and sufficient for knowledge must reflect the character of the virtue.

Thus if, initially, we say: knowledge is constituted by the believing of a true proposition, with justification that evinces a certain causal pedigree; we are in effect proclaiming that knowledge is a good that is both enjoyed (possession of true information) and deserved, or earned (justified, according to standards of causal propriety). We may then expect the conditions of justification imposed on genuine knowledge, with their accompanying causal conditions, to reflect or conform to the magnitude of the intrinsic good. Yet this magnitude is *emphatically* not an empirical quantity, to be sought out and measured by observation and subsequently delineated in terms of criterial requirements (e.g., of a minimum amount of justification). Rather, argumentation in favor of some specified set of criterial requirements must proceed much on the order of moral reasoning. Moreover, I wish to put forward the view that some epistemological inquiry just is a special case of moral inquiry, incorporating a process of reasoning about values that are not empirical.

Truth doesn't vary in degree whereas justification and causal propriety do. Let us concentrate, for the present, on justification. The amount and kind of grounds for a belief may vary greatly, and it is the concern of epistemology to specify a standard minimum of justification: of the various possible degrees to which a true belief may be grounded or justified, what is the lowest level of justification needed to warrant it as knowledge? We entertain an imaginary conflict regarding sufficiency of justification.

One disputant, D_1, claims that S_1, a subject, knows that her own son, B, was born in the month of February. The subject's justification of her belief, if typical, is obvious—she remembers the date on which she bore her son. The second disputant, D_2, claims that another subject, S_2, also possesses knowledge of the same proposition. S_2 is acquainted with B, however his ground for his belief happens to be that another person, whom S_2 regards as truthful and fairly reliable, told him that B was born in February and that he (the informant) had obtained the information from still another person; and S's informant had provided him with no assurances as to the second person's reliability. Disputant D_1 dissents from the truth of D_2's claim: S_2's belief, maintains D_1, is not sufficiently well justified to pass for knowledge. D_2, on the other hand, insists that S_2 is justified, even though he would not be if there was a longer chain of informants along which the information had to pass to reach S_2.

Who is right? Patently, D_1 is right about S_1's belief—this is a clear, unproblematic case. But is D_1 right about D_2's being wrong? *Apparently*, but not *obviously*, so. It would be highly unreasonable to deny S_1 her knowledge, but it would not be nearly so unreasonable to grant S_2 his. Although I do not think that S_2's cognitive condition is a genuine borderline case—i.e., I think that it's *moderately* clear that S_2 does *not* know that B was born in February (unless he has other grounds!)—still, the adequacy of S_2's grounds is much less a clear case, and much more a matter of contention, than S_1's case. Since S_2 indeed has *some* grounds for his belief, it is not incoherent to hold that he has enough; but it would require proportionately more (and craftier) argumentation just to maintain it (to say nothing of convincing others).

Thus the example of the D_1–D_2 dispute illustrates that *adequate* justification is a matter of being justified to a certain degree and in a certain way—not merely a matter of having some *grounds* for belief. What that degree and that way are, is not an issue to be settled empirically but rather must be decided normatively. To inquire just how it is to be decided normatively, then, is extremely appropriate, and I shall attempt to sketch an answer, omitting some important detail.

As a preliminary exercise, let us focus upon the reciprocal relationship between the intrinsic value of knowledge and the degree of justification that knowledge exacts of the believer. In general, the greater the stringency of the justification requirement, the more exalted will be the intrinsic value of knowledge that meets the specified standards. This is because, the more the requirement excludes, the more difficult of attainment knowledge will be. But more importantly, not only the stringency, but also the *form* of the requirement, will be influenced by a theorist's intuitive conception of *what kind* of a good or virtue knowledge is—just as moral intuitions are brought to bear upon ethical principles. One particularly interesting dimension, along which marked intuitions of one or another sort may be expected to be experienced, is that of individual autonomy or responsibility. In fact, the autonomy theme will occupy a prominent place in much of the remainder of the present chapter. It is concerned with the question just how independent of others a subject must be in the justification of his beliefs—or, with regard to the grasp of propositional components, how independent he must be in certain relationships with the extramental world.

Knowledge is frequently attributed to a plurality of subjects collectively, with no clear intention of attributing to each individual in the group the justification that would be required of an individual knower singly. For instance, the statement "On the morning following election day, the Americans knew that Reagan had been returned to office" may be true within a certain language game, even if it was not true of every individual American independently that he/she knew that morning that Reagan had won. Suppose yourself to have been among the small group of Americans who did believe, the next day, that Reagan had won again, but without good reason—rather, as the result of hearing a rumor begun early the previous day. Nevertheless, in the language game I am discussing you do share or participate in this knowledge, qua member of the group, as the group "justifies your belief for you." There is, of course, a serious question about the legitimacy of drawing this inference (that each member possesses the knowledge attributed to the group) from a collective attribution of knowledge—although the practice of collective attribution hardly seems objectionable in itself. Recall the dispute between D_1 and D_2 about whether subject S_2 actually knew that B was born in February. The inference from collective attribution to singular attribution, if legitimate, would authorize attributing knowledge to S_2, in the following way: If S_2's informant's informant was justified in believing (i.e., *knew*) that B was born in February, then, because S_2's own informant held the belief, the plural attribution of knowledge to the two informants would be correct, and so would a plural attribution to a group including S_2, thus by collective-to-singular inference, affording S_2 knowledge without justification.

There are two kinds of intuitions at work here. First, I have recorded an intuition about a particular case of purported justification: it seems, on reflective examination, that S_2 is not justified in his belief. Also, I have brought out—albeit implicitly—an intuition on a basic theoretical orientation: a subject should be held responsible for the justification of his own beliefs, and treated as an autonomous agent. Both kinds of intuitions may contribute to the development of acceptable principles (here, principles of justification), and to the rejection of inadequate principles that may be proposed. It is naturally conceivable that others may repudiate my intuitive views on these matters; yet it is significant that the intuitive observations I have presented cohere with each other, and I shall show that they fit together in symmetrical fashion with still other such observations.

While still on the topic of knowledge, it is instructive to contemplate briefly one of the causal requirements among principles of justification, and the role of intuition in motivating it. A causal requirement—or a more abstract requirement that implies it—should be imposed for the purpose of avoiding Gettier-type difficulties, as suggested by Goldman and others. The suggestion is roughly that the truth of the proposition believed must figure causally in the subject's belief; less roughly, that the event or state of affairs by virtue of which the proposition is true, causally brings it about that the subject believes that proposition. Being causally responsible for the subject's belief, that state of affairs must also figure causally in the belief's grounds or justification. The Gettier problems themselves are based upon the intuition, in each case, that the proposition in question is not *known* by the subject. That the subject fails to have knowledge in a certain case in which he has a true belief, is not an observable fact, but a matter of judgment. And similarly, the supposition that a causal connection is needed appears to be intuitive, in the attempt to solve Gettier's query.

The grasp of propositional components can be accorded a treatment parallel to that of knowledge: it is immune to naturalism because such grasp is an *acquaintance* with elements of the extramental world, and acquaintance—as contrasted with merely being in a psychological state of a certain type—also carries a sui generis intrinsic value to be acquainted with an individual, or a property or relation, is cognitively intrinsically good. It involves a knowledge of a part or parts of the world—only *not* propositional parts. Furthermore, in componential grasp there is a correlate of justification, and a correlate of the causal condition on knowledge, neither of which can be settled by empirical inquiry. These elements we shall explore in the next section. Thus the parallel between grasp and knowledge will be reinforced, as well as the overarching epistemological hierarchy.

It is important to notice that there are two realms that cognitive theory, which includes both theory of knowledge and theory of content, is concerned with. One is a purely psychological realm, and the other a moral or value-theoretic realm. Neither theory of content, nor theory of knowledge (which contains it) is located wholly within the psychological sphere. For the purpose of sharpening this distinction, we may recognize a distinction between two kinds of subjectivity, and (in a sense) two separate kinds of subjects. I shall refer to "the psychological subject" as distinct from "the epistemological subject" or "the moral subject". The latter two are identical, as the epistemological subject is an embodied subject-agent in the world, just as the ethical subject is, and, like the ethical subject (agent), is an entity of which we are primarily interested in predicating values of certain sorts.

2

This section is primarily a study of the architecture of cognition, elaborating upon the nature of the two hierarchies mentioned above, that of grasp and that of knowledge. I shall follow a methodological course of seeking a high degree of structural parallelism between these two ordered series; but without forcibly imposing unnatural forms for the sole end of the parallelism. The levels of the upper hierarchy, that culminating in propositional knowledge, will be discussed first. General principles will be sought, concurrently, to define each level or transition between levels. These principles will be, in so far as possible, articulated in such a way that they may be applied equally well to the levels of the lower—the "grasp"—hierarchy.

Knowledge may be stratified in either of two different ways. In either case, belief {1} is the "ground floor," the lowest level. All knowledge entails belief: more properly expressed, knowing that P involves believing that P. The other elements in knowledge are justification of belief {2}, truth of what is believed (the content) {3}, and a special condition {4} some one of a set of conditions designed to meet Gettier's objections. The quandary about stratification, however, lies not in the choice of {4} but in the question whether the main stratum intermediate between knowledge and mere belief is to be defined by truth {3} or by justification {2}. If by truth, then the second level, that which is directly above belief, is the level of true belief belief which may or may not be justified. If the latter, the second level is the level of justified belief—belief which may or may not be true. If we allow justification to define the second level (i.e., adopt the scheme {l-2-3-4}), we will have chosen to allow this level to be defined by a principle that is as "internal" as (i.e., no more externally determined than), belief itself. On the other hand, if we let truth define the second level (thus: {l-3-2-4}), it will be defined by an "external" principle. Preferable to allowing an "external" level to be sandwiched between two "internal" levels, would be to suppose the principle of transition between belief and the second level to be "internal," and to let this second stratum be the level of justified belief. This option I shall call the option of *internal stratification*, and the other that of taking the second stratum to be the level of true belief I shall call *external* stratification. Thus we adopt the internal of the two options and it will be generalizable to the grasp-hierarchy, and preferable within that hierarchy for the same reasons that it is in the knowledge-hierarchy.

It is noteworthy that the level of belief, the bottom stratum of the upper (knowledge) hierarchy, has traditionally been portrayed as internal to the subject, i.e., as psychological in character. We might consider sustaining this portrayal as a convenient fiction, but then again, it would ultimately be highly misleading. Yet we do now have a piece of conceptual apparatus that will empower us to salvage the traditional "inner" flavor of belief without compromising theoretical correctness. Belief can properly be said to be internal to the epistemological subject, while failing to be internal to the psychological subject.

Each step in the hierarchy can be cast as genus-cum-differentia. Belief itself consists in entertainment of a proposition conjoined with judgment that the proposition is true. For the purpose at hand it is not necessary to dwell on the nature of judgment, but merely to acknowledge it as an element in belief—specifically, the differentia, or feature differentiating it from mere entertainment. The next transition, that from belief to justified belief, is somewhat more difficult to specify. Accordingly, I shall be quite vague in my characterization since, after all, the primary object is to present a rough outline of the stratified structure common to both grasp and knowledge. A belief is justified via a relation in which it stands to other beliefs and to perceptual episodes. It is important that justification is a matter of a structure or relationship that is internal in the same respect in which belief itself is internal. The relationship is typically an inferential one (though certainly not invariably strictly deductive), and its exact nature is a normative concern: standards of justification are matters of value rather than of fact. Furthermore, it is reasonable to impose standards of justification that vary with the subject matter: e.g., we may expect that more be required (viz., deductive certainty) by way of justification of mathematical beliefs than by way of justification of common-sense beliefs about the external world. This content relativity of justification would seem to detract from its internal status. We shall return to examine this puzzle subsequent to some discussion of the lower hierarchy and its top stratum—the grasp of propositional contents and their components.

At this juncture the external world enters inexorably into the cognitive architecture. To the genus of justified belief we add the differentia *truth*. On the traditional analysis of knowledge, this combination forms the top stratum: knowledge itself. But Gettier's problems demonstrate that another stratum {4} is needed, either immediately above, or directly beneath, that of justified true belief. I shall explore three different possible differentiae, corresponding to three alternative resolutions of the Gettier difficulty. The first of these resolutions is due to Goldman, who places a causal condition on justification. To circumvent the Gettier problems, he claims, it is, essential that the following condition be fulfilled: the fact (i.e., truth) of the believed proposition P must be appropriately causally connected with the subject's believing that P (i.e., with his being in the psychological state that he is in, that in fact realizes his believing that P). Goldman spell out the *appropriateness* rudimentarily in terms of perception, memory, and causal chains of certain sorts. One option, then, is that we add the differentia "appropriately caused," together with Goldman's elucidation (or the equivalent), to the genus *justified true belief*. Clearly, the new level must occur *above* that of truth, as the truth of the proposition is presupposed by the condition itself.

A second condition to be considered is due to Lehrer, who locates the source of the Gettier troubles in the "transmission" of justification through one or more false propositions. Lehrer proposes, therefore, that knowledge, besides involving belief that is true and justified, demands that all propositions essential to the justification be true; or, as he himself expresses it, that "[t]here is no *F* that is false and such that if *f* were doubtful for *S*, then *S* would not be completely justied in accepting [*P*]." So one alternative to the causal condition is to take as differentia the stricture against false propositions occurring essentially in the belief's justification. The decision whether to fit this additional stratum between justification and, thrugh (thereby designating it the third level) or directly above truth (as the fourth and highest level) is in this instance largely arbitrary. Let us conventionally assign it to the topmost position; this will be convenient for the third possible solution as well.

The third solution, Nozick's, is another alternative to the causal theory, and, like Lehrer's solution, utilizes a counterfactual condition. Nozick includes as a necessary condition of knowledge, that if the proposition believed were *not* true, the subject would *not* believe it. This third possibility for the differentia of the top stratum, like the other two, deals adequately with Gettier's problems. Which of the three possibilities is to be preferred to the others, depends chiefly upon how applicable the principle in question is to the lower hierarchy. For example, despite the difficulties inherent in the causal theory, Goldman's proposal—as representative of this family of theories—seems to adapt itself to the grasp-hierarchy with greater facility than does Lehrer's principle. (Nozick's, in turn, is better adaptable than Goldman's, and without the disadvantages of the causal theory.)

The task now is, wherever possible, to employ the differentiae that define the strata of the upper hierarchy, in defining correlated strata in the lower. In some cases it may be advisable to amend the principles' formulations in favor of increased abstractness. We begin with the first level in the lower (indeed, also in the combined) hierarchy, that of psychological states—not total psychological states, but partial, or sub-states. Of course there is no principle we use to define the class of entities on this level by reference to those on lower strata: simply because there are no lower strata. It is the transition between the first and second levels that must initially be characterized, and by an analogue of justification.

Justification of belief may be depicted, roughly and basically, as a relationship between the belief to be justified, on the one hand, and a set of other beliefs and related entities (such as perceptual episodes) on the other. The one belief in question derives support from the others. As conjectured above, the support is usually inferential, but not exclusively deductive. In seeking a differentia that will apply within the content-grasp hierarchy in addition to the knowledge hierarchy, it is prudent to try out a principle more generic than that of inference, examining whether it is suitable within the realm of psychological states. To this end I suggest—deliberately remaining vague and intuitive for the moment—the concepts of coherence and support. From a set of propositions, another can be inferred *only if* it coheres with them and is supported by them; and typically only if they cohere with each other (except in such cases as reductio inferences). All of this appears rather less than significant unless one considers representing justification (and not just inference) as a *species* of coherent support (of justificandum by justificans). The grounding of one piece of information *in* a body of other information obtains by virtue of the support provided by that body (note the metaphor of resting on or against), and the coherence of the new piece of information with the old (notice here the notions of integrity and *mutuality* of support). Let us therefore attempt to define the second stratum of the grasp hierarchy, taking the first stratum as genus and the idea of coherent support (or supportive coherence, if you like) as differentia. It is important that this be *internal* coherent support in order to maintain the parallel with the knowledge hierarchy. The question of adequacy of the definition, then, is the question whether from the initial stratum, that of psychological states, we can through the application of a concept of this sort as differentia, obtain a second stratum that, in its own hierarchy, occupies the place of justified belief in *its*. (Also, of course, whether there is any psychologically or philosophically explanatory *use* for such a stratum.) Setting aside for the moment the question—an extremely important one—what exactly the first stratum "looks" like, consider certain ways in which such a second level must stand related to the first and to grasp itself (the fourth). In the second stratum may be expected to be found psychological states that are appropriately related to sets of other psychological states. States on the second level must be as "internal" as those on the first. Hence they cannot *require* for their determination or specification any reference to the extramental world. (Naturally this is not to stipulate that, were we in a position to specify them we could not even informally, for the sake of convenience, refer to one of them as, e.g., "the inner concept of water", etc.) And, toward a more positive characterization, we may bear in mind that at the next stage we add the analogue of *truth* to obtain states of the moral subject-agent that are only (modulo Gettier-insurance!) minimally different, at most, from states of full-fledged grasp or competence.

Thus, what we find in the second stratum are psychological configurations (not total, but partial psychological states) that are the *solipsistic constituents* of the grasp of cognitive contents. Remember that the chief entities being grasped are properties, relations, and individuals—and propositions constructed from these along the lines of a Russellian or Barwise-Perrian semantics. What we grasp are emphatically *not representations* of these propositions and their components, but are the components and propositions themselves. We might be truly said to *represent* them, which is the same (or nearly) as to say that we grasp them; but this differs from the idea of grasping *representations* of them.

What constraints upon the nature of psychological states per se, the first-stratum denizens, have we? Unfortunately few enough so far, besides their narrowness and their role in a cognitive theory of behavior. Yet we may take a cue from Fodor and endeavor to develops speculatively, some of their expectable characteristics.

For our purposes, there are two possible ways a viable narrow psychological theory might turn out. The first is Fodorian. Assuming, as we are wont to do, that *something* about our beliefs, desires, etc. is causally efficacious, we find it natural to believe—as the Fodorian sanguinely does—that psychological state-types will be discovered to be, *in any fixed physical and social context*, correlated exactly (1-1 onto) with pairs consisting of an attitude and its content. The "discovered to be" must here be unpacked as "postulated as theoretical constructs in a maximally general and economical narrow theory". Thus in our physical environment and linguistic community, there would be exactly one psychological state type such that being in a state of that type is to believe that oceans contain water. Although Fodor himself seems not to explicitly acknowledge the context-relativity, the view is in a "language of thought" vein. On Twin Earth, this same state type would constitute (better: underlie) the belief that oceans contain *xyz*. We might call this the "Just Add Water" view: that given a basic psychological state type, all that is required for content (and attitude) determination are the relevant contextual factors (in this case, the reference of 'water') Note here that sensory images and memory images may be admitted as Fodorian states, since they bear semantic content too, and are type-individuable in a way orthogonal to the way their contents are classified.

The non-Fodorian side of the MS coin is the counsel of skepticism. To achieve a maximally universal and economical theory of cognitive psychology, it is doubtful that relations to Fodor's de-semanticized representations will do the job as basic state-types—they may simply turn out to be too coarse—although there is no reason not to expect that they will be expressible as equivalence classes of complex configurations of whatever types of states turn out to be basic. The main point is: they will not have semantic contents as such, because their syntax will be wrong.

Let us suppose that Fodor is wrong about the texture of the most adequate narrow theory; and that hence that theory must admit state types that are too finely individuated to sustain semantic interpretation. One way of imagining this state of affairs is to suppose that there is a "language of thought" whose sentences are syntactically *further decomposable* than sentences of natural languages. Thus syntactic units such as predicates and terms, which are in natural language not decomposable into any more basic syntactic elements, might be so decomposable in the language of thought. These more basic elements would defy any semantic interpretation using natural language as a metalanguage, since the metalanguage would lack the requisite syntactic and semantic *categories*. Clearly such a theory would have to be preferred to any conceivable wide theory since the finer texture would achieve a higher degree of explanatory and predictive precision than the Fodorian texture: presumably it is just this superiority that it may have over its Fodorian rivals. Furthermore, there can be no quasi-naturalistic (wide) counterpart to such a theory.

We should expect the development of non-Fodorian narrow theories especially given the current popularity and fecundity of computational conceptions of the mind and the fine-grained texture of many computing languages. Assuming that they do develop, then at least the major part of cognitive psychology must be methodologically solipsistic, not on a priori, but more on empirical grounds. Whether it turns out to be the case that narrow psychology is Fodorian or not, it can still be argued that internal organization of psychological states is essential to the grasp of propositional components, and so that the second stratum—defined by reference to support and coherence, is a level that must be of interest to cognitive theory.

For assume that the Fodorian view is true. If so, the grasp of any propositional component is underlain by a separate psychological state of a certain type. Thus there is a psychological state type, to be in which, on Earth, constitutes the grasp of the content *water* (i.e., H_2O), and to be in which, an Twin Earth, constitutes the grasp of the content *xyz*. That state, because of its inescapable syntactic properties, must be intimately related to other grasp-underlying states, in virtue of syntactic interactions of sorts; this is not to say that the states themselves interact, but that the possession of syntactic properties suggests the use of syntax by some entity or other. Invoking the language of thought paradigm, the psychological state which underlies the grasp of an individual, property, or relation in the world, is a state of competence with respect to a term or predicate in the language of thought. (In most instances, too, the grasp itself is correlated with a state of semantic competence in the use of a term or predicate in a natural language.) A psychological state of this variety constitutes an inner, or solipsistic grasp; the grasp of an "inner content." Such inner contents are not grasped in isolation, however, by any means.

Inner meaning must be systematic—i.e., inner content is conditioned by the place it occupies, and the role it plays, in a system. Consider the inner meaning corresponding to the semantic content (i.e., the property of being) *human*. This inner content is the content that it is partly in virtue of the support it derives from other inner contents in the system of acceptance (roughly, the solipsistic counterpart of belief). Thus inner content is rendered coherent, in large part through its occurrence in mentalese sentences that are rationally accepted by the subject. The majority of English speakers, for example, accept the sentences "Humans are animals," "Most humans are rational," "All humans are mortal," "I am a human," etc.; and of course other sentences that make statements less central to the meaning of 'human'.

The fact that these are rationally acceptable mentalese sentences, that express (what we should call) solipsistic, or inner, propositions containing the inner content *human*, attests to the *coherence* of that inner content. On the semantic ("outer" content) side of the coin, all propositional components must be coherent: they must be capable of occurring in propositions that can be rationally believed, or whose negations can be rationally believed. There simply are no graspable semantic contents that are incoherent, since in a situation of purported grasp of an incoherent content, there would be nothing to grasp: all real contents (individuals, properties, relations)—as well as some that are not actual—are coherent. They are delineated by the ideological schemes in which they are found coexisting with other contents. A propositional component thus depends for support, upon other contents with which it may combine to form coherent, entertainable propositions. The possibility of incoherent components is excluded by the necessary coherence of complete propositions (which, of course, to be coherent, may not contain any *components* that are incoherent). It is through propositional networks whose thread is logic that propositional components support each other, and through similar counterpart networks that the psychological states that are their solipsistic counterparts lend mutual support.

To summarize: if narrow psychology is Fodorian (in the special sense enunciated above), then the feature of coherence is essential to psychological states underlying the grasp of propositional components; this coherence consists in systematic support lent by other states (which themselves underlie grasp and belief); and it is essential because a related kind of support is required by the semantic contents themselves. (Note that this renders the Fodorian view, as I have stated it, false, since more than extramental reality is needed to obtain a semantic content from a psychological state. However the spirit of this view can be preserved via an obvious amendment of its formulation.)

Now suppose, which is more likely, that narrow psychology turns out not so simple in its taxonomy of causally relevant state types; that *not every* coherently supported psychological state will determine a semantic content (propositional or componential), relative to a given extralinguistic context in which the subject is situated. Yet the argument for a coherence condition adapts easily to this eventuality for we might still, If we wished, deal with Fodorian types of states. The only difference is that they would not be *basic* types, and might, for psychological-explanatory purposes, appear quite artificial. Each token state of a Fodorian type would be realized by a *configuration* of basic states, although other tokens of the same type could be realizable by distinct configurations. But given any such configuration, underlying the subject's grasp of a content, the same need for coherent support arises because it is inherited from the corresponding need in the semantic realm. Here then, we have groups of states supported by other groups of states, rather than mere *individual* states supported by groups.

There is another good reason to conclude that the grasp-hierarchy has as its second stratum a region defined by i) psychological states with articulate structure that are ii) coherent by reason of being "supported" by other such states. Again the strategy involves an appeal to a parallelism between the grasp-hierarchy (having as top level componential acquaintance or competence) and the knowledge-hierarchy (which has propositional knowledge as top level). We are seeking two further strata for the grasp-hierarchy: one an analogue of truth and the other an analogue of the Gettier-antidote that we settle upon as final or topmost differentia in the knowledge-hierarchy. Nozick's condition, we shall see, will be preferable—in large part *because* it has an analogue of the appropriate kind, which is better suited to the problem of grasp than the others.

Deferring the discussion of the resolution of Gettier-problems and their counterparts, let us fix the truth-analogue so as to be able to justify the coherence-level through its relation to the next level up since the truth of a proposition pertains to a certain type of situation obtaining in the world, we are naturally led to what we might call *actuality* as an analogue of truth, or even as a genus that includes truth as a species. If, with Fodor, we take psychological states to be relations between a subject and a bit of syntax (an expression in the language of thought), actuality in the realm of grasp may be characterized as follows: a coherent, articulate psychological state exhibits actuality iff there is an individual, property, or relation in the world to which the bit of syntax involved in that psychological state refers.

The second principal argument for the inclusion of coherence in the grasp-hierarchy turns upon the parallel between the relationship of justification to truth, on the one hand, and that of coherence to actuality, on the other. Justification has the characteristic that we may call "*truth-seeking*": a belief that is justified is more likely to be true than one that is not justified. This is why we are more likely to believe a proposition asserted by someone else if that person provides *reasons* for us to believe it. And in general, a rational person is more likely to believe any given proposition that he entertains if he has evidence for, or reason to believe, that proposition. The evidence, or supporting information, is presumed true, and the appropriate rules of inference are known to be valid. Now coherence, among articulate psychological states (states that are candidates for bearers of grasp), stands in the same relationship to actuality, as justification does to truth; we express this relationship by saying that coherence is "actuality-seeking." A component-representing state that is coherent, i.e., supported by other such states, is more likely to have a referent in the world, than one that is not. (Of course, the probability of an incoherent state underlying the grasp of an actual semantic component is nil—as implied in part of the foregoing discussion.) A coherent state carries the presumption of actuality, for it is suported by other states that are presumed to exhibit actuality.

The differentia of each stratum, in both the grasp-and the knowledge-hierarchies, is essential to grasp and knowledge respectively; in that, in the absence of any of these specific conditions, grasp or knowledge fails. Thus, for example, one cannot *know* a proposition that is not true, nor can one's belief constitute knowledge if that belief is not justified. In the grasp-hierarchy, the first differentia, analogous to justification, is coherence. What goes wrong if a subject's purported grasp of a semantic content is incoherent? How or why would the subject fail to grasp any content in such a situation? To address these questions, it is first necessary to sharpen the notion of coherence somewhat. From a positive point of view, the coherence of a content underlying state is its support by other content-underlying states—and this support is of the sort that, given the inner contents associated with the supporting states, the inner content of the state in question is clearly fixed. From a negative perspective, the lack of coherence of a state amounts either to its lack of definite inner content, or its involvement in a contradiction.

If a psychological state purporting to underlie the grasp of a semantic content is incoherent it must be because the subject does not accept enough sentences of mentalese (again to employ that Fodorian conceptual framework) constructed from the relevant psychological state and other supporting states, i.e., such that the relevant inner content is adequately supported by others; or because the mentalese sentences accepted by the subject are inconsistent. As a blatant example of the latter, inconsistent variety of incoherence, a subject S may accept both the mentalese equivalents of "Dana is a man" and "Dana is a woman," and in addition, that of "No man is a woman," leading to the contradictory "Dana is *not* a man." It is easy, likewise, to construct examples in which the subject intends to refer to a general content—a property or relation—but fails by reason of inconsistency. Besides incoherence that is due to logical inconsistency, there are also instances of incoherence due to *insufficiency*. A subject may accept the mentalese equivalent of "The color indigo falls between blue and violet on the spectrum" yet fail to be in a psychological state that refers to the color (property) indigo, since the acceptance of that sentence is the *only* support for the state purporting to refer to indigo (and, moreover, the person cannot recognize instances of indigo by sight.) Again similar cases of insufficiency can be conceived for states that purport to refer to individuals.

The incoherence of a psychological state that purports to underlie the grasp of a semantic component precludes that the subject grasps any such component by means of that state, just as absence of justification pecludes knowledge. As justification is the subjective contribution to knowledge, given a believed proposition; so also is coherence the subjective contribution to grasp, given a psychological state of a certain (viz., articulate) kind. (Justification may, indeed, be regarded as a species of coherence: coherence in both forms is concerned with rationality it is less than fully rational to attempt to hold an unsubstantiated belief, or to attempt to conceive a propositional component in isolation from other such parts of the real world.) In the question of grasp, coherence is the minimum required by way of *internal* assurance that one's psychological state has semantic reference. On the knowledge side, justification is the minimum required by way of internal assurance that one's belief is true. We must depart slightly from the strict parallel between the two hierarchies, however, in allowing that a lack of justification does not entail falsity of belief, even though it seems that a lack of coherence must entail that the psychological state in question fails to refer. Contrapositively, if a psychological state refers, then it is coherent; whereas the truth of a belief does not imply that it is justified.

Next we must consider actuality and truth as differentiae of their respective strata. The chief question within the grasp hierarchy is, *Should there be a stratum defined by the principle of actuality?* Or, alternatively, Is it essential to the grasp of a propositional component, that component be actual? Since the question of *existence* of concrete individuals is metaphysically clear-cut and unproblematic, as contrasted with questions of actuality of properties and relations, let us first address that part of the issue pertaining to concrete individuals. What must be determined, then, is whether it is necessary for an individual to exist, or to have existed in the past, in order for a subject to cognitively grasp that individual as a semantic content. An affirmative answer is most commonly and convincingly substantiated through a premise maintaining the indispensability, to such grasp, of a *causal connection* of a certain kind obtaining between the individual and the relevant psychological state of the subject. The nature of this connection is difficult to specify precisely, but this connection, or something like it, is necessary, in the knowledge-hierarchy, for the avoidance of Gettier-type problems. It has been pointed out that difficulties are generated by the attempt to include a causal condition in an *analysis* of knowledge; but other, more plausible remedies for Gettier problems—notably Nozick's approach—are, it will be argued, best *realized* by a causal mechanism of sorts in fact, one of a sort that warrants the form of actualism at issue.

Problems with grasp, that are like Gettier problems in the sphere of knowledge, will lead us to the recognition of a necessary condition for grasp, that is analogous to Nozick's condition on knowledge. This too will be seen to be realized by a causal mechanism: the subject's grasp-underlying psychological state being appropriately caused by (among other factors) the individual that is grasped. It might be added that if that individual has had no causal efficacy in the production of that state, it is difficult to see how his grasp can properly be held to be of *that* individual rather than some other—i.e., how that individual can properly be the referent of the state. And of course, if the individual has causal powers, it must certainly exist, or must have existed in the past. Hence actuality would seem to be requisite to the grasp of individuals.

Properties and relations must be divided into two different categories because they exhibit two different kinds of actuality. For simplicity's sake let us call these categories the a priori and the empirical. Among the empirical properties and relations we shall have to consider both the simple and the compound. The a priori category corresponds to the class of inner contents discussed in this section above—those which are simultaneously inner and semantic.

It would be useful, eventually, to devise a definitive formula for distinguishing between a priori and empirical contents—but for present purposes it is inessential. It suffices to have an intuitive conception of the distinction that empowers us, when presented with a content, to make a reasonable judgment as to which category it exemplifies.

Clear cases of a priori properties and relations are (among others) *circular* and *identical to*. These contents are inherently actual because they are imposed on the world, as it were, by the mind. Their criteria of individuation proceed from the understanding, hence they need not appeal to the external world for the definition of their content as empirical contents must. Since these inner contents are simultaneously "outer" (i.e., semantic) contents, and are grasped just by virtue of their coherence, they need not be instantiated in the physical world in order to possess actuality. It is a significant feature of these contents that they need not be made known to us through a causal chain originating in their instances.

Properties and relations that are *empirical* contents (with some notable exceptions; see below) may be labelled actual only for a different reason—viz., because they have instances in the physical world. Natural kinds are the paradigm case here. Contents such as *gold, magnesium, cat, rhinoceros,* are contents that could not be grasped if they did not have instances. In the realm of relations we might find such empirical contents as *redder than,* and *brother of.* It is not just the coherence of the inner counterparts of these contents that defines them, and sets them apart from other possible semantic contents; rather, it is also the fact of their instantiation in the actual world. Thus the *actuality* of such properties and relations, requisite to their grasp, consists in their having instances. As with concrete individuals, it is reasonable to think that there must be a causal connection between actual parts of the world and the relevant psychological states of a subject if those states are to underlie the grasp of properties and relations exemplified by those parts of the world. In fact, as will become somewhat clearer, the grasp-hierarchy's analogue of the Gettier antidote in the knowledge-hierarchy itself entails the actuality of contents that are grasped, and it is possible—but not necessary—that this entailment proceeds through the entailment of a causal connection. I.e., either the analogue of the Gettier condition must work through a causal mechanism, which in turn entails the actuality of the causes, or else that condition itself (directly) entails the actuality of the relevant contents.

A priori contents might most advantageously be viewed as *formal* contents. This is why, although they are capable of being instantiated in the physical world, the only actuality that they require in order to be grasped is their coherence. This is what is meant by their *inherent* actuality. Empirical contents, on the other hand, not being purely formal, are in part extramental, and their very actuality is contingent: such a content need not have been *available* in the world to be grasped. Again, the very possibility that the psychological state underlying the grasp of *water* might as well have underlain the grasp of some other (albeit similar) substance, underscores this point.

Within the category of empirical properties and relations, a problem arises in connection with contents that are explicitly compounded from other properties or relations. Some such compound contents may clearly be grasped (provided that they are coherent) even though they are obviously not instantiated. For example, the content *orange raven* is easily understood, i.e., grasped, although there are no orange ravens in existence, nor have there ever been. Yet by grasping the component contents *orange* and *raven* separately, we understand the compound content as well. Hence for the case of compound properties and relations, it is advisable to insist that, provided that the compound is coherent (which proviso excludes contents such as *square circle*), its actuality derives from the actuality of its components. If it is coherent and its components are actual, then the compound itself is actual.

Turning, finally, to the highest stratum of the grasp-hierarchy, we must ask how a certain state—an articulate psychological state, supported by others, that seems to refer to an actual semantic content in the world—can fail to constitute the grasp of the indicated content. i.e., what can go wrong if we do *not* add the analogue of a Gettier condition as a final differentia? Consider a scenario inspired by Putnam's paper: A Twin Earthian "transported" to Earth is in a psychological state that fits just those descriptions, and the state he is in seems to constitute a grasp of *water*. The appropriate isomorphism (or homomorphism) exists between his psychological structure and the world, which would lead one to believe that the relevant state refers to water. However he fails to enjoy a grasp of the content *water*. What he grasps is clearly something else; he *mistakes* water (*our* water, H_2O) for this other stuff—and this is additionally perplexing because he calls that other stuff "water". Analogues of Goldman's and Nozick's requirements for avoiding Gettier problems can easily be formulated for the grasp hierarchy by substituting "psychological state" for "belief" and "actuality" for "truth." Along the lines of Goldman's solution, we may stipulate that the psychological state must be appropriately caused by the actuality of the content in question. Alternatively, following Nozick, we may require that, in order for grasp properly to obtain, the psychological state in question would not exist if the content were not actual.

In the realm of knowledge, Nozick's condition (that if *P* were not true, then *S* would not believe *P)* is superior to Goldman's causal condition. Both succeed in avoiding Gettier-type counterexamples, but the causal condition presents some serious complications that Nozick's condition seems to be free from. The most notorious of these is the difficulty involved in specifying adequately the necessary *appropriateness* conditions: the phrase 'appropriately caused' could be construed in just about any way, but no single construal presents itself graciously and claims truly to accommodate all cases accurately. One problem, arises with general contents—properties and relations. These contents can hardly be held capable of *causing* anything, of bringing anything about themselves—even a psychological state—in the way that individuals and events are thus capable. Then, too, there is the objection that "the relation between knowledge and causation is not a necessary truth" (Lehrer, 1981, p. 77) and hence that the causal condition has no part in an *analysis* of knowledge. (This I take to be incidental, however; because, although an analysis of knowledge is to be desired, it is not my primary objective here to produce one.) It is not difficult to see how Nozick's condition, on the other hand, in each case of knowledge —contingently—gets fulfilled or carried out by means of some causal relationship or other. This would explain the attractiveness of the causal condition, while simultaneously suggesting that Nozick's counterfactual condition is behind (as it were) the general tendency for the causal correlations in question to occur.

To see that Nozick's condition does indeed rule out the Twin Earthian's grasp of *water*, note that in the case described, the condition does not hold: it is *not* the case that if water were not actual, he would fail to be in the (token) psychological state that *appears* to refer to water. In this situation, he would still be in that state by virtue of his grasp of *xyz* on Twin Earth. If he did grasp the content *water*, the condition would have to hold. And, in fact, it holds for *xyz* (which he calls "water"): he would *not* be in *that* (token) state if that chemical substance were not actual on Twin Earth. (We should say, strictly speaking, that he grasps nothing by means of that state here on Earth, since *xyz* is not actual here. The very thought of inter-world, travel is confusing, and probably not fully coherent!)

Two points must be emphasized here. First of all, that we are officially adopting Nozick's approach rather than Goldman's in the matter of "Gettier-proofing" both hierarchies. The former certainly is simpler, more elegant, easier to formulate in an acceptable way, than the latter. Secondly, however, we shall continue to be very interested in the *causal* connections that are so important—for our purposes essential—to knowledge and grasp. These connections, together with networks of coherence or justification, will illuminate our consideration of the *abilities* associated with knowledge and (particularly) grasp. We will consider the ability to pick out or re-identify which is associated with grasp, and which is practically *derivable* from the notions of coherence and the causal connection, and a constitutive principle of individualism that we shall adopt.

Finally, the reason the causal condition appears to be implied by Nozick's counterfactual condition is that if an ostensibly grasp-underlying psychological state depends on the actuality of the ostensibly grasped content, it seems that this dependency must be causal in nature: that if the subject would not be in that state but for the actuality of the content, it is because the content itself is somehow causally responsible for the subject's being in the state.

3

In the previous chapter the thesis of narrow psychologist, in cognitive theory (NPC) was discussed and dismissed. NPC is an individualistic doctrine, in that it amounts to the complete determination of cognitive—i.e., semantic—contents by the states of the individual subject who holds those contents. It has been emphasized that, on the contrary, in addition to the psychological states of the subject (which must, to fulfill meta-scientific desiderata, be systematically individuated in narrow, or methodologically solipsistic, fashion), the character of the world itself—specifically those parts or aspects of the world that the attitudes in question are *about*—must figure in content-determination as well. Furthermore as Burge (1977) has pointed out, social or conventional boundaries of concepts (e.g., those of the concept *arthritis*) usually make a difference to contents held.

The species of individualism we have repudiated is especially strong. A suggestive synonym for NPC is 'Strong Cognitive Individualism', as it is the thesis that the state of the individual subject is the sole determinant of content. By contrast, there are several weaker species of cognitive individualism—positions that ascribe to the individual subject various degrees of contribution to the determination of cognitive contents. I wish to espouse one such species of individualism in particular, and shall call it simply 'Weak Cognitive Individualism' (WCI). This is a position that is, arguably, implicit in our system of cognitive attitude attribution. It proceeds from certain moral/epistemological ideals, such as those of individual autonomy and responsibility. Roughly expressed, advocating WCI will involve our according to the (internal) psychological state of the individual *as great a contribution* to the determination of content as possible; and, equally importantly, denying the subject any sort of grasp or knowledge "by proxy" (such as is implicated in certain relations of what has been called "epistemic dependence" (Hardwig, 1985). Although interesting in its own right, WCI will be shown to lead to a highly significant necessary condition on the grasp of semantic components: viz., the epistemological subject-agent's ability to recognize a content in its actual occurrences in the world.

The hierarchies we have developed for epistemology and content theory may very well provide an analysis of each of the key concepts—grasp and knowledge—but conceivably they may fall somewhat short of delineating sets of severally necessary and jointly sufficient conditions. This is of minor importance to the primary focus of the project in which we are engaged. This project is motivated by the rejection of narrow psychologism. In rejecting NPC we are, in effect, asserting that the elements determining the contents that are grasped or held by a subject are both internal and external in nature—just as the elements essential to one's knowledge of a proposition, *as ordinarily conceived*, are both internal (belief and justification) and external (truth and a Gettier-antidote). The point of constructing the dual hierarchy is to draw a picture of the constellation of types of elements entering into content determination, by reference to, and analogy with, the elements of knowledge. The picture, not coincidentally, is meant to arrange these elements in the order of their respective internality or externality. The stipulation of the parallelism is a methodological guideline for obtaining basic constraints on, and necessary conditions for, grasp, from the structure of knowledge. In fact *grasp*, also known as *acquaintance,* is every bit as much a genus of knowledge as is propositional knowledge.

Observe that the fact that belief itself is not properly internal suggests that a certain measure of re-definition of the strata in the knowledge hierarchy will be appropriate if we intend full parallelism between the two hierarchies. The differences between viable possibilities of ordering—and the differences between the accompanying definitions of the separate strata—are significant indeed. Our adoption of the doctrine of WCI, and the related effort to preserve a high degree of individualism by preserving the maximum internal contributions to the major epistemic phenomena (grasp and knowledge), must constrain—and justify—the choice of definitions and orderings that we ultimately make. By the same token, the fundamental thrust of WCI can be advantageously explored by comparing a pair of different possibilities of stratification.

Near the opening of the foregoing section, the possibility of (what I labelled) "external stratification" was broached. Although it will be clear that very little plausibility attaches to this option, let us consider it in the interest of illuminating one of the salient features of WCI. External stratification allows an external element to enter into the hierarchy already on the second level. Consider the knowledge hierarchy, independently of whether or not a breed of external stratification can be defined for a grasp-ordering. First, the bottom stratum is that of belief, and belief is (naively) taken as an entirely internal state. In the external scheme, however, the next two levels are permuted. Truth is the second here, and justification the third level; the highest is, as before, defined by a Gettier condition (although *which* one is not immediately germane). Two necessities—1) the externality of the conditions of a propositions truth, and 2) the requirement that no transition from one level to a higher is a transition defined by a differentia more *internal* than the immediately preceding one—given that truth is the differentia of the second stratum., dictate that justification, as the differentia of the third level, be construed completely externally. With a modicum of reflection it is clear that the second condition is reasonable to adopt, in the spirit of WCI, as a more formal statement of that doctrine, which is directly pertinent to the construction of the epistemic hierarchies. To achieve maximum internal contribution to content it is imperative to avoid adulterating internal principles with external—i.e., to avoid the inclusion of any ostensibly internal principles that in actuality contain an external factor.

What happens, then, if justification, entering on the third level (subsequent to truth) must be construed as fully external. Prima facie, this construal does not appear altogether ludicrous. Given that justification is a relation holding between beliefs and other (sets of) beliefs, a similar (but "external") relation might be held to obtain between *true* beliefs, on the scheme of external stratification. The natural choice for such a relation, since the standard justification relation is one of internal support, would be that of *implication*, i.e., an external species of support.

Not much perspicacity is needed in order to feel the dissonance between this view of justification and our ordinary conceptions of belief, justification, and knowledge. Justified false beliefs would be ruled out, thus barring subjects from *failing*, in a peculiar but important way, to enjoy knowledge. On our received view, knowledge may fail through no fault of the subject—if the subject holds a justified belief, but something else goes wrong (such as, typically, that the proposition fails to be true). On the other hand, in the external scheme, unjustified true beliefs would be possible, and the subject would not be *responsible for* the failure of knowledge in such cases; yet under our ordinary conception of knowledge and justification, he *is* responsible. So it grows increasingly apparent that to diminish the sphere of internal participation in knowledge would amount, at least in this case, to a diminution of the autonomy and responsibility of the individual subject. Ruling out justified false beliefs deprives us of the autonomy involved in occupying an intermediate epistemic state that is of moral value in itself, without depending for this state upon physical or social conditions in the external world. Again, if justification were construed purely externally, the subject would be deprived of the *responsibility* attendant on such autonomy: that of being responsible for the justification of his beliefs—the failure of which is important whether the belief itself be true or false.

The untenability of external stratification results from our subscription to certain epistemological principles (notably value principles) that are inherent in our ideas about knowledge and its attribution, and that provide strong support for WCI. The latter can be paraphrased as the thesis that grasp and knowledge are to be constituted as thoroughly as possible by the (internal) psychological states of cognitive subjects, and correspondingly as little as possible by circumstances external to the subject. Adherence to this thesis has profound consequences for the architecture of cognition. The principles of cognitive autonomy and responsibility entail WCI. It has been shown that the structural alternative of "external stratification" is entirely unsatisfactory on the grounds that it would severely limit the degree of cognitive autonomy enjoyed by individual subjects, as well as the responsibility that may be imposed upon them. These two principles are deeply ingrained in our moral/epistemological conceptual schemes. The internal stratification alternative is warranted by WCI because it consigns an indispensable ingredient of knowledge—viz., justification to the psychological realm, thus insuring that the internal contribution to knowledge is appropriately greater than it would be on the alternative arrangement.

Before turning to arguments for the truth of WCI, it is valuable to explore just how WCI constrains and dictates the structures of the cognitive hierarchy. Generally speaking, it must dictate that all contributions on the part of the extramental world, to knowledge and grasp, must fall into categories that appear in the hierarchy only after all the categories of psychological contributions have appeared. We are led directly to a compulsory metamorphosis; a simplification and integration of the hierarchies as they have been developed thus far, in accordance with this primary dictate of WCI.

A problem arises with the designation (hitherto) of *belief* as the first, the ground-level stratum, in the knowledge hierarchy. Belief has been widely, uncritically taken as a wholly internal, or psychological, phenomenon. We now know that this is patently false on the methodologically solipsistic approach to psychology which I have adopted. Belief places the subject in a relationship with a proposition, hence with the extramental world. On that first stratum, then, there would occur an implicit contribution by the world. But something is indeed amiss, since at that level, not all the relevant internal contributions have been made. Justification itself, the differentia of the next stratum up, is essentially internal in character. It is important that the support-relations involved in justification are relations among psychological states primarily, and only secondarily (and almost incidentally) relations among propositions that are contingently associated with those states. To characterize justification as a relation holding between one belief and a set of one or more others, is to miss the point that the crucial support relation occurs at the inner, the methodologically solipsistic, level. Thus we have, in the original version of the knowledge hierarchy, a violation of WCI .

The obvious task is to construct a knowledge hierarchy that has the psychological states that underlie beliefs, rather than beliefs themselves, at its ground-level stratum. This will automatically alter the position of the knowledge hierarchy relative to the grasp hierarchy. To conceive the former to be vertically superimposed upon the latter would run counter to WCI too, as an internal level would then succeed an external level. And, supposing that we let states of *acceptance*—those articulate psychological states underlying beliefs—form the foundation of a new knowledge hierarchy; the next stratum up would presumably be that of *justified* acceptance, to which then it would seem natural to add the differentia *truth* in order to obtain the penultimate stratum. The second step, justified acceptance, is plausible enough, but it is a perplexing matter, how *truth* can be predicated directly of (justified) acceptance. It makes no sense, in general, to speak of true acceptance, since the object of acceptance is not a proposition. (Employing the "acceptance" idiom, we might find it convenient to shift to a language-of-thought idiom—without, however, committing ourselves to the substance of any such theory—and so to declare that the objects of acceptance are mentalese sentences. This notion of acceptance will then deviate but little from Perry's. What appears to be needed here is an intermediate level of justified belief, between justified acceptance and justified true belief. The new hierarchy might thereby come to resemble the old in its top strata.

There is no such simple expedient to be had, of merely inserting another stratum; and perhaps this is fortuitous. It turns out that we shall have to fuse or collapse the two hierarchies together horizontally The main clue pointing to this necessity is that, even if an intermediate level of justified belief could be inserted directly above that of justified acceptance, certain elements of the *grasp* hierarchy— notably coherence and actuality—would need to be introduced in order to make the desired transition. It looks improbable that there is any way to circumvent the steps bringing these elements in. *Grasp* is indispensable to belief (though not to acceptance), and grasp requires at least these two elements. Indeed, to get to belief, it looks as though *all* the elements of the grasp hierarchy must be recruited. Now it remains to be demonstrated that a *joint hierarchy* is possible, one moreover that respects the dictates of WCI.

Each stratum of the original grasp hierarchy corresponds to exactly one stratum in the original knowledge hierarchy. We may take each of these pairs as a single level in the composite hierarchy, but with the minor modification noted, viz., that of specifying states of acceptance as the ground level on the knowledge side. Each stratum may be divided into a *sentential* side, accounting for the appropriate level of the knowledge hierarchy, and a *componential* side, accounting for a level of the grasp hierarchy. The division between the second and the third strata is the important line of demarcation between the internal and external contributions to the cognitive phenomena, i.e., the psychological and the extra-mental constituents of grasp, belief, knowledge, etc. It is of the utmost importance that arrangement abide by the dictates of WCI. To see that it indeed does, we shall trace the constitution of grasp, belief, and knowledge of semantic contents, noting that once the line is crossed—i.e., once extra-mental constituents are introduced—no more internal elements need be added. Thus in each case we shall consider a progression: not a temporal or developmental, but rather an architectonic progression, from basic psychological states to full-fledged cognitive phenomena.

We begin with a study of the grasp of a propositional component. For the sake of simplicity, let us choose a content like water. On the first stratum there is an articulate psychological state which involves an uninterpreted representation, or at least something *like* a representation. (I shall consider the status of representationalism, and its ontological implications, presently.) On the second level, that of coherence, the sentential side of the two lower strata plays an essential role. The subject must be in psychological states that may (for the sake of convenience) be described as the acceptance of mentalese sentences containing that representation which, when interpreted, is a representation of water; together with other (uninterpreted) representations, each of *which* has its place in the bottom stratum, on the componential side. For the coherence of the water-representation to be legitimate, each of the accepted sentences must be justified—i.e., supported—by one or more other sentences. In acceptance, too, there is an element of *judgment* that must not be overlooked: it is certainly possible to *understand*, in the narrow sense, a mentalese sentence without (again in the narrow sense) *assenting* to it. This variety of assent is intimately connected with justification, for if the subject is rational, he will withhold assent (hence judgment) in the absence of justification There is, in this internal half of the hierarchy, obviously an intimate interanimation of compartments. Of these compartments there would seem to be not *four* (defined by basic states and support in one dimension, and componentiality ad sententiality in the other) but in fact *five*: two strata on the componential side and three on the sentential; the concept of judgment is applicable only unilaterally, viz., to sentential forms. Because of this interanimation, the vertical ordering of these strata is only partial, and so it may appear a trifle odd to speak of a stratification. Nevertheless we must label the various compartments the only distinction thus far remaining to be made explicit is that between acceptance and the non-judgmental psychological states underlying acceptance. These latter we may call "bracketed entertainment" for want of a more facile expression. Both bracketed entertainment and acceptance should be conceived as belonging to a single, more inclusive stratum, which may be (loosely) referred to just as "acceptance."

The effects of the extra-mental elements in componential grasp may now take their respective places. Actuality attaches only to the representation in question: it is necessary that *it* refer. Yet the situation would be quite anomalous if many of the supporting representations failed to refer. The representation of *phlogiston* may have been one item in a support-reticulum at one time without single-handedly invalidating the grasp of the referents of those items to whose support it was contributing. However with a number of different non-referring representations in supporting positions, it would be difficult to concede that grasp truly occurs. To complete the componential grasp, it must be the case that the subject would not be in the psychological state in question if there were no actual denotation (in this case, if water did not exist).

The grasp of a complete proposition is next to be considered. Requisite to such grasp is the grasp of each of the components of the proposition. However in tracing the structure of the grasp of the whole we must proceed in a manner that does not involve descending back into strictly internal levels after any external elements have been introduced. Hence rather than describing the phenomenon by proceeding to the grasp of the whole by way of synthesis of the grasps of the parts, the synthesis must be described as occurring on the internal side of the line of demarcation. So again, beginning with the psychological states that underlie the respective componential grasps, each of these is supported in a reticulum of accepted mentalese sentences (to invoke the language-of-thought model again merely for convenience of exposition), each of which presumably has some justification for being held. The mentalese sentence which underlies the proposition whose grasp we are interested in, need not *itself* be accepted, however. The entertainment of the proposition that water is a major chemical constituent of the sun (for example)—and the bracketed entertainment that it rests upon—is certainly feasible without any commitment to the truth of the proposition, thus without the *acceptance* of the corresponding mentalese construction. Beginning, then, with the psychological states underlying the various componential grasps, we cross the vertical line separating the componential from the sentential realm; finding in the latter, on the lowest stratum, the sentential psychological state which is a synthesis of these componential psychological states and which underlies the grasp of the proposition. External contributions to the grasp of a proposition pertain only to the propositional components. Actuality attaches to the (coherent) *componential* psychological states: the proposition need not be true, but its components must be actual. Similarly, the only Gettier provisos to be imposed, are imposed on the respective componential grasps: the subject would not be in the respective psychological states were it not for the actuality of the components.

Hence to trace an instance of propositional grasp the order that must be followed is i) psychological states underlying grasp of components of the proposition; ii) synthesis of these to form a psychological state underlying the grasp of the proposition itself; iii) acceptance and justification of mentalese sentences containing the bracketed components, such that each of the sets of sentences forms a reticular structure bestowing *coherence* on its componential psychological state; iv) actuality of the components; and v) the counterpart of the Gettier condition, applied to those components: that if they failed in respect of actuality, their respective psychological states (bracketed grasps) would fail to obtain. Let us attempt now to trace the belief of a proposition in similar fashion, with strict observance of the WCI constraint. This will be a remarkably easy task, now that the sequence constituting propositional grasp is at our disposal. All that needs to be added is sentential *acceptance* at the psychological level: all else remains the same as in the propositional-grasp sequence. A step may be inserted either between ii) and iii) or between iii) and iv) in this sequence—namely, the acceptance of the mentalese sentence assembled in ii). Justification, though not a necessary element in belief, is usually concomitant upon such acceptance.

Finally, propositional *knowledge* may be traced within this composite proportional hierarchy. To belief we must attach justification, truth, and the counterfactual Gettier condition. Justification consists in the sentence or psychological state's being *supported* logically by one or more others. It occurs immediately above acceptance in the psychological arena. Truth belongs in the stratum of actuality, but on the sentential side. Since truth is of the extramental category, it is an element that must be added only subsequently to all mental contributions—preferably even after the two external elements on the componential side. Lastly, the Gettier condition follows upon the heels of truth: if the proposition were not true then the subject would not accept the underlying mentalese sentence. (Note that acceptance is critical in the Gettier condition and is purely internal: the psychological state that is caused by the truth of the proposition is *not* that of mere bracketed entertainment, but the stronger state of assent to the sentential entity).

This composite hierarchy, through which it is feasible to trace instances of cognition of any of these four prominent kinds, has been designed to isolate the entire body of internal contributions to content and attitudes, from the extramental factors that figure in their determination. For the purpose of normatively assigning to this total internal body the greatest weight in relation to the external factors (consonant with WCI), it is essential to adopt a framework which effects such an isolation. In other words, the character of the cognitive hierarchy, its constitution and structure, serves an important purpose: that of enforcing WCI. By isolating the categories of internal contribution, thus forbidding any admixture of external factors in then, we have appropriated the power of decisiveness for then. Their relative weight can be increased *independently* of the weight of the external factors.

This idea of maximization of weight of the internal contribution can—and should—assume two different, but closely associated, meanings. First of all, the campaign to establish WCI as a doctrine and working principle of the anatomy of cognition, is concerned with strengthening and shaping the *requirements* that are placed upon the internal states and processes of the subject. An increase in the demands upon the individual subject above and beyond those recognized by positions inimical to WCI (either fancied or actually espoused), is the fundamental aim of this campaign. Thus in one sense, the maximizing of the relative weight of the internal factors consists in making the demand (and presumably, making it plausibly) that the standards of grasp and knowledge be modified in the way of increases in the requirements imposed upon internal factors—requirements of both degree and kind of contribution. Secondarily, we concern ourselves with the actual compliance with these more stringent requirements, in instances wherein knowledge or grasp, belief, etc. are alleged to occur. This compliance will manifest itself predominantly in the form of coherence and justification that are more thorough, less assailable, and more extensively conducive to certainty and firmness of grasp. About such compliance—on the part of actual cognitive relationships, with the revised demands for maximum relative weight of the internal—more will be said below. We must first inquire into the revisions that are to take place.

The activity of revising the standards of relative weight of the internal contributions to grasp and knowledge, is a felicitous example of epistemology in its normative role, in action. Epistemology should not be a merely descriptive activity; and those doxastic theories and theories of knowledge are most edifying, which engage in a certain amount of idealization, elevating the standards and criteria for these phenomena beyond the normal standards to which we typically adhere in our actual everyday practice of cognitive attitude attribution. Conformity to the letter of our actual attributional practice, them, is not a desideratum: rather we wish to pursue the *spirit* of that practice to its logical conclusion, which, although perhaps extreme, is by no means absurd or ridiculous. The salient feature of that "spirit", for our purposes, is a strong *individualism*. The following are some themes to be borne in mind while exploring this individualism. Firstly, knowledge and grasp, and belief, are indeed goods—i.e., positively valued qualities—of the individual to whom they are correctly ascribed. Secondly in the attributional paradigm, the individual subject is viewed and treated as a moral agent: the subject is an individual, with two notably related properties that are partially constitutive of individual moral agency; viz., autonomy and responsibility. Thirdly, WCI is the natural elaboration of this individualism.

Contained in the foregoing considerations is a transcendental argument, or at least the rudiments thereof, for the doctrine of WCI. An implicit individualism is inherent in, and essential to our (rather deeply entrenched) attributional framework. Before pursuing this line of argument further, it behooves us to examine the two most important ways of denying WCI—two antitheses or *foils* of WCI. Both involve particular ways of denying the autonomy that WCI entails, and so the advantage gained will be an increased understanding of WCI and of the steps to be undertaken in its defense. The first of these foils is a scheme exhibiting a simple disproportion of dependency on the environment in the determination of attitude and content. The second is due merely to a special case of the malady evinced by the first, consisting of an undue dependency upon the *social* environment. Let us consider an example of how, pursuant to the first of these foils, a subject might be accorded a lesser degree of responsibility than WCI demands. Given a definite description, 'the first male child born in New York City in the year 1920', a subject may hold a belief that whoever fits that description lived through the Great Depression. The description itself is an easy one to master cognitively. It would seem to be within the individual sphere of competence of nearly every competent English speaker. But the knowledge of, i.e., the acquaintance with, that person who in fact satisfies the description, is another matter completely. In order to hold *de re* attitudes about that person, such acquaintance is necessary, and (from the standpoint of WCI) is not immediately consequent upon a competence with respect to the description from the point of view of the "environmental foil," however, the environment—rather than the subject himself—makes the necessary connection, and by reason of the actuality in hand, the *de re* competence automatically accompanies the descriptive competence. The "social foil" is similar. Here an increment of grasp or knowledge is allowed solely on the strength of another subject's possession of that grasp or knowledge. Suppose that subject S_1 is well acquainted with a person—say Professor W. Sellars—at time t, but that subject S_1 is not. At time t_2, S_1 makes reference to Prof. W. Sellars in conversation with S_2. Thereafter, according to this "social foil", and contrary to the dictates of WCI, S_2 also enjoys *de re* grasp of Prof. Sellars, in virtue of the contact with S_1 and *his* grasp of that person.

Although the examples cited pertain just to *grasp*, and to the absence, in these foils, of (some of) the *coherence* prescribed by WCI, the situation with knowledge, and hence justification, is similar. Parallel examples can be constructed, but need not be at this point: the purpose for which the foils were invoked has been served; the two principal kinds of autonomy mandated by WCI have been identified, as a) freedom from the environment in general, and b) freedom from one's social surroundings, in the relationships of cognitive support.

The remainder of this section will consist of 1) a recapitulation and augmentation of the line of argumentation followed thus far in favor of WCI. This argument has been predicated upon an assimilation of epistemology and cognitive theory to value theory. The justifiability of the normative idealization undertaken is maintained on this ground. In revising the concept of knowledge through idealization from the spirit of our attributional practices and paradigms, we emphasize the exalted *value* of knowledge (and here under knowledge I mean to subsume *grasp*, as a special case, as well). We acknowledge higher standards than in the ordinary conception, thereby rendering the genuine article somewhat more difficult, though by no means impossible, of attainment nor even prohibitively expensive—and hence by the same token, more worthy of the *effort* involved in such attainment. The intent is not to assume an elitist posture toward knowledge, but nonetheless is to demand and reward persistently reflective and inquisitive habits of mind.

Autonomy and responsibility of the individual subject-agent are fundamental ethical values. The moral paradigm of the individual is *constituted* in large part by these characteristics. They are properties that must be ascribed to any individual capable of being the subject of moral praise or blame. They are not virtues earned or acquired by subjects individually, but rather properties that are imposed on the individual by the moral framework itself. This must be the case with the conceptual framework of any sphere in which *individuals* are ascribed states deserving of praise or blame. Thus if the *paradigm* cognitive attitude attribution is inherently individualistic, i.e., if the paradigmatic ascriptions of cognitive attitudes, *qua* states possessing value and disvalue, are ascriptions *to* individual subjects, or at least ostensibly so—then these individuals, in virtue of their individuality, must be, constitutively, both autonomous and responsible. And this certainly is the actual state of affairs: the attributional framework decidedly is individualistic in this regard. This we know from the usage of verbs of attitude ascription and their typical entailments. *Collective* knowledge or grasp is not prior, but the reverse: in ordi-

nary practice, ascription of knowledge or grasp to an individual subject does not presuppose an underlying knowledge or grasp on the
part of a group to which the subject belongs; yet attributing a cognitive attitude to a group *does* entail that (some, at least, of) the
individual members of the group enjoy that attitude by themselves.

It is worthy of note that the control, the autonomy at issue,
resides in the inner, the psychological subject; and that the subject's
exercise of this control—i.e., that activity (largely of ensuring, in so
far as, adequate support relationships) for which the subject is held
accountable—is quite independent of the facts of the subject's situation in the world. Nevertheless it is only in virtue of being so situated that a subject is capable of holding properly cognitive
attitudes—of grasp, belief, or knowledge of semantic contents. We
may thus recognize a sense in which the inner subject is the subject
of cognitive attitudes primarily and essentially; and the situated subject—the epistemological subject—is the subject of these attitudes
only contingently or derivatively. We may attribute genuine semantic contents only to a situated subject (epistemological subject, or
subject-in-world), but the emphasis in attribution is on the contribution of the subject, *not* the world. The fact that an attitude is held
has to do directly with the psychological states of the subject in that
adequate support, which is essential to both grasp and knowledge,
is an internal matter. What the *content* of the attitude is, however, is
a function of the subject's situation in the world. Two varieties of
approbation and disapprobation may be distinguished: one of these
directs attention only to success or failure of grasp or knowledge
due to internal control (or lack thereof) and without regard to the
semantic content involved; the other variety directs its regard to the
content as well. So a subject may be held in esteem merely for having exercised sufficient control to succeed in grasping or knowing
something on a certain occasion—or may be held in contempt for
failing to exercise the requisite control. On the other hand, one may
praise a subject for his success in grasping (knowing, etc.) some

specified content *C,* or may condemn him for failure to grasp (or know) *C.*

Higher degrees of support—i.e., coherence and justification—and the markedly internal character of this support, are the earmarks and primary manifestations of a cognitive theory espousing WCI. The "foils," the antitheses of WCI discussed above, are decidedly anti-individualistic in substituting external support for internal—in not only tolerating, but insisting upon, the adequacy of certain brands of external support, e.g., the contingent identity of a certain object with the denotatum of a certain description mastered by the subject. In the interest of autonomy and responsibility, then, no reliance on external means of support—*in lieu* of internal support—is allowable: for this would be support over which the subject would lack control, thus undermining his autonomy; and for which he (therefore) could not rightly be held responsible. An additional point at issue, besides the *quality* of support, is its *quantity.* WCI dictates not merely that coherence and justification be internal in nature, but that they be strong enough for a putative instance of grasp or knowledge to succeed. Strength, or *breadth*, of support is intimately connected with its internality. In the matter of justification, a non-individualistic theory may require only that the acceptance of a sentence of mentalese rest upon the acceptance of another such sentence, that expresses a proposition which happens to be true, but whose acceptance in turn need not be justified. But individualism requires that the justification of any acceptance that is not foundational, be a logical dependency not only upon something else that is also accepted, but upon something else that is accepted and justified as well. Thus, in accordance with WCI, the justification of one accepted sentence may involve a long line (or more probably a tree like sequence) of justified acceptances.

The question of degree or extent in the case of coherence, as a requisite element in grasp, may be viewed in a somewhat different light. It will be argued presently that WCI, within our framework of strata, implies that legitimate grasp involves a specific ability, on the subject's part, to recognize or identify individuals that are grasped, as well as instances of general contents that are grasped. This ability admits of degrees, to which degrees of *coherence* (in its positive aspect of interanimation of states) more or less closely correspond. And clearly, individualism will demand a greater, rather than a lesser, degree of both. Yet the demands will not be so stringent as to preclude the possibility of genuine grasp, or elevate it beyond the reach of the moderately well mentally-equipped subject. The extent of coherence required for the grasp of a given content, although dependent on the nature and level of difficulty of the identificatory ability that is required, will not exceed normal mental limitations: for the abilities required will be far from perfect or total, and their minimum extent will be determined by other considerations. Recall that coherence was cast as interanimation of consistent psychological states and sets of states; and similar to the case of justification, WCI entails that a state is supported by others that cohere with it, only if those others are themselves sufficiently well supported to be judged coherent.

By way of summary, the reasons for accepting WCI can be stated as follows:

1) Our attributional paradigm is individualistic: we attribute grasp, belief, knowledge, and other cognitive attitudes primarily to individual subjects. It is also *individual* knowledge and understanding that is primarily valued. We tend to think in ideal terms of grasp and knowledge as cognitive states that individual subjects are as individually responsible for as possible. The support-relationships, which are the focus of the responsibility, we tend to view (in the attributional paradigm) as wholly internal.

2) Knowledge and grasp that meet the standards imposed by WCI are not only attainable, but probably also extremely common. (Of course if WCI is accepted, *all* authentic knowledge and grasp, to qualify as such, must meet its standards.)

This is to deny that external support—relationships are ever *necessary* to grasp or knowledge; which should be further seen as a reason to deny that they can ever be *sufficient*. 3) This is because we are obliged to impose the highest standards that *can* be met, commensurate with the high value placed upon grasp and knowledge. Predictably, this must mean the highest *individualistic* standards, due to the very nature of our attributional framework.

Under the auspices of WCI, much of what commonly passes for grasp—i.e., competence with respect to propositional components must be dismissed as illegitimate by reason of its reliance upon external modes of support. To reject such phenomena as irrevocably worthless would of course be to disrupt our normal attributional practice to the point of obstructing its practical utility. It behooves us therefore to concede a second-class status to these phenomena, and keep ourselves apprised of their *relativity* to external contributions of support. This form of relativity is avoidable, and it compromises individualism (and internality of grasp). Speaking precisely, then, we may recognize "quasi-grasp" (and similarly, "quasi-knowledge", although most of our inquiry to follow will focus upon grasp) and cultivate an awareness of its various species, and of its propensity to "contaminate" the grasp of larger packages of content in which occurs a "quasi-grasped" bit of content. The proper grasp of a composite will, as a rule, require propriety of grasp of all its individual components.

Another, less insidious, brand of relativity is discernible in the grasp of cognitive contents. Unlike relativity to external support, this variety is unavoidable and does not erode the individualistic paradigm. To characterize it, a consequence of WCI together with our cognitive hierarchy should be examined. WCI prescribes a coherence that ensures meaningfulness of those states that underlie grasp of cognitive contents. These states must be internally well supported, although the extent of the support that is appropriate may vary with the type of content; but in any case the reticular structure must be such as to *locate* conceptually the state in question. It must be linked logically with other states underlying the grasp of propositional components, and ultimately, with patterns of sensory stimulation. It is important that there be a background of successful grasp, against which to locate a given state. Major flaws in the background (e.g., due to improper connections with the extra-mental world) will tend to undermine the legitimacy of grasp of any content purportedly grasped via the state under scrutiny.

References

Bach, Kent [1982] *De re* belief and methodological solipsism, in Andrew Woodfield, ed., *Thought and Object* (Oxford: Oxford University Press).

Barwise, Jon and John Perry [1983]. *Situations and Attitudes* (Cambridge, Mass.: The MIT Press, A Bradford Book).

Burge, Tyler [1977] Belief *De Re*, *The Journal of Philosophy* LXXV.

Fodor, Jerry [1980]. Methodological Solipsism Cnsidered as a Research Strategy in Cognitive Psychology, *Behavioral and Brain Sciences*, 3. Reprinted in *Representations* (Cambridge, Mass.: The MIT Press, 1981).

Gettier, Edmund [1963] Is Justified True Belief Knowledge?, *Analysis* 23, no. 6.

Goldman, Alvin [1967] A Causal Theory of Knowing, *The Journal of Philosophy*, LXIV.

Hardwig, John [1985] Epistemic Dependence, *The Journal of Philosophy* LXXXII.

Kaplan, David [1968]. Quantifying In. *Synthese*, 19. This volume of *Synthese* was reprinted with minor changes as Donald Davidson and Jaakko Hintikka, eds., *Words and Objections* (Dordrecht, Holland: D. Reidel, 1969).

Lehrer, Keith [1981]. Self-Profile, in Radu J. Bogdan, ed., *Keith Lehrer* (Dordrecht: Reidel).

Nozick, Robert [1981] *Philosophical Explanations* (Cambridge, Mass.: Harvard Univeristy Press).

Perry, John [1979]. The Problem of the Essential Indexical. *Nous*, 13. Reprinted in *The Problem of the Essential Indexical and Other Essays* (New York: Oxford University Press, 1993).

Putnam, Hilary [1975] The Meaning of 'Meaning', in Keith Gunderson, ed., *Language, Mind and Knowledge* (Minneapolis: University of Minnesota Press).

Quine, W.V. [1956] . Quantifers and Propositional Attitudes, *The Journal of Philosophy*, LIII. Reprinted in W.W. Quine*The Ways of Paradox, and Other Essays* (New York: Random House, 1966).

Russell, Bertrand [1929]. Knowledge by Acquaintance and Knowledge by Description, in Bertrand Russell *Mysticism and Logic* (New York: W.W. Norton).

Schiffer, Steven [1978] The Basis of Reference, *Erkenntnis*, 13.

Name Index

B
Bach 27, 35
Barwise 12
Brentano 47
Burge 6, 27, 30, 31, 80

C
Carter 50

D
Descartes 17

F
Fodor 18, 19, 20, 21, 22, 23, 25, 32, 34, 35, 36, 48, 54, 67, 68, 69, 70, 71, 72, 73

G
Gettier 44, 59, 60, 61, 63, 64, 66, 71, 75, 76, 77, 78, 79, 81, 82, 89, 90
Goldman 59, 63, 64, 78, 79

H
Hardwig 81
Husserl 47

K
Kaplan 6, 27

L
Lehrer 64, 79

M
Meinong 11

N
Nelson 50
Nozick 64, 71, 75, 78, 79, 80

P
Perry 10, 12, 20, 86
Plato 45
Putnam 18, 27, 28, 29, 30, 31, 32, 33, 37, 44, 78

Q
Quine 1, 4, 5, 6, 7, 8, 32, 48, 54

R
Reagan 58
Russell 10, 11, 13, 27

S
Schiffer 27